Almost A Gentleman

Almost A Gentleman

A Personal Story of a Soldier in WW2

James David Leek

Copyright © 2008 by James David Leek.

| ISBN: | Hardcover | 978-1-4363-2400-7 |
| | Softcover | 978-1-4363-2399-4 |

All rights reserved. No part of this book may be reproduced or transmitted in any form or by any means, electronic or mechanical, including photocopying, recording, or by any information storage and retrieval system, without permission in writing from the copyright owner.

This book was printed in the United States of America.

To order additional copies of this book, contact:
Xlibris Corporation
1-888-795-4274
www.Xlibris.com
Orders@Xlibris.com
47839

CONTENTS

Prelude 9

Chapter 1: One Zillion and One 13
Chapter 2: Infamy to Unknown 15
Chapter 3: In The Army Now 19
Chapter 4: Moving On 23
Chapter 5: Whoopee 31
Chapter 6: Finally Delivered to Buffalo 34
Chapter 7: The Dream Is Over 47
Chapter 8: Convoy Across the Atlantic 61
Chapter 9: In Not So Jolly England 63
Chapter 10: Crossing The Channel to Le Havre 67
Chapter 11: Headlong Into Battle 70
Chapter 12: The Voyage Home 89
Chapter 13: The Countdown to the Finale 96

Some thanks are due

First — I owe a great deal to my wife who has heard these stories a thousand times and still can smile when I ask her to remember names and places. She also put up with my struggles at the computer and was (and is) a tough but accurate critic. My thanks and Love to her.

Second — Thanks to our kids and kidlets who also have heard these stories more than they want, but still keep saying "Keep going".

Third — All of our friends have said they would read every word. Now what could be better than friends like that?

Finally — Thanks to our Daughter in Law for rescuing my document from the depths of the delete well. And to our Daughter who used her time and graphic skills to put everything together, do the cover design and make all the whimsical changes I suggested.

Prelude

My father's generation was the best generation of all. It became extremely clear to me on September 11, 2001 as terrorism struck the fabric of our nation. My father concurred with me when I called after the events of 911 that the atrocities were very similar, if not more devastating than the events of December 7, 1941, that day known as Pearl Harbor. My father and his generation went to war to fight for our entitlement after that day. That entitlement was for us. Their war was more bloody than ours has been so far. My father carries the pain and scars to this day, every day. And yet, every day, he still shows the gentleness of spirit, pride and the determination that has made him the man that he is. What my father's generation brought home to us was our entitlement of what we have in freedom, choice and a chance for the ability to do what we can dream. My father and his generation have entrusted us to carry on that entitlement to teach the values fought for by their actions to our heirs, such things as life and human value, honor, respect, sacrifice and opportunity. It is our legacy. It is our promise and our gift to our heirs.

I have not yet read the memoirs that my father is writing today about his childhood, his upbringing or his war he fought for us. I do know that what is underlying is his words that he is passing down to us, are the values of my legacy. I hope I learn them well.

Douglas Leek

November 26, 2001

Jim and Dee,

The last page of Jim's autobiography was read yesterday. I must say, "I really, really enjoyed reading it . . . Every page!" Not only did I learn many new facts about you both, but it gave me a new insight of Jim Leek. You certainly have had an interesting life. "Interesting" is not a word that describes the fullness of your life, but a word that would fit won't come to me. The people you have met (and kept in touch with), the places you have been (and still remember), the hard time and the good times, and especially the character it all built.

The section on the war was almost overwhelming. I grew up during the "air raids" and watching the war news at the Saturday matinee, but reading your first hand experiences was at times too close for comfort. I can only imagine what it was like for you to remember those things and write them down. It had a profound impact on me. Although, I have always stood proudly for the "Stars Spangled Banner", from now on I will stand straighter and prouder.

I encourage you to write that novel. Your experiences need to be shared!

I talked so much about your "book" that Don has now decided to read it, so it will be awhile longer before you get it back.

Hope all is well and have a great day! And, thanks for entrusting your book to me for awhile.

Love, Jean

Chapter 1

One Zillion and One

This starts on December 7, 1941. But as you will no doubt point-out, there are a zillion stories starting that same date. So we will just say that this is one zillion and one!

It really started early morning of June 7, 1924 in Lebanon, Mo. when I made my debut into this world. Mother said it wasn't so bad. Dad said he had never had such a hard time. That probably proves something, but I am at a loss as to what.

Dad was a station agent and telegrapher on the Frisco Railroad. I was brought up around depots and trains. The other part of my life was small town living and a love of the woods that were so much of a part of the Ozarks. The woods are still there, but not as many trees as I remember. Progress does take its toll on the innocent pleasures of the mid 1920's. I could go into the woods alone with no fear of being molested. I could shoot off my .22 rifle (which I received from my Dad) in any direction without fear of hitting a person. I could bring home rabbit, squirrel, quail and grouse to supplement the food that was grown in our garden or bought from the small stores. Along with the always present pigs, chickens, geese and ducks, we were self sufficient.

Dad lost his job on the railroad when I was 11 because he had the gall to speak up for a local Republican who was running against the Son of a State Democratic Senator. He in turn was a relative of the person who ran the Frisco Railroad in Missouri.

Our good life was changed.

For nearly a year I helped Dad with the chores. We took care of the livestock. I learned how to use a two man bucksaw to saw down trees and how to use a double bitted axe to chop the trees into wood for the cook stove and heating stove. It was hard work but necessary.

We finally found ourselves in Kansas where Dad was able to put his skill of telegraphy to work in the office of Cities Service Oil. The oil did not smell nearly as good as the trees of the woods we just left, but it did provide us with a living.

My academic career until I graduated from High School in 1943 was not wonderful. Besides the regular classes, I took two extra subjects and one extra activity which do stand out, at least to me. The extra activity was learning the trombone and playing in the school marching band. The trombone followed me into the war which I will be discussing later. One of the subjects was typing of all things. I was the only male in the class and took a certain amount of ribbing from my friends. But throughout my life I have made good use of this skill. I used the typewriter for class assignments and later on was able to write scripts for broadcasting that did not have to be written over. And now in the computer age I can sit here doing this writing and not worrying about whether or not it is legible—only if it makes sense. The other subject was speech. The class was taught by a Mr. Henderson, a tall slender man who originated in England. He was the typical Englishman of the movies, pencil mustache and all. He had a talent for turning a high pitched Kansas twang into a reasonably apt speaker. This was something I have used over and over during my life. It is absolutely necessary to be able to speak clearly and correctly.

My math was wasted with a class taught by a Mr. Smith, a sour old guy that hated all the boys and loved all the little girls. It took me years to catch up on what I could have learned in that class.

Chapter 2

Infamy to Unknown

But that was all left behind on December 7, 1941.

We were in the kitchen of the little house in Oil Hill, Kansas that morning, listening to the small radio that sat on top of the ice box. I was 17 at the time and both Mother and Dad looked at me and I know now what was going through their minds. Another year and I will be in the thick of it.

The next day the Principal called a meeting of all the students and he and several of the older teachers took turns talking to us. Mostly they admonished us to take it easy and don't panic. The one I remember most was a History teacher who said, "We live in a great country, with great resources and a strong will. We must put our minds and bodies to work to bring these hoodlums to justice".

With these words of what turned out to be great wisdom we set our minds to the task at hand. And I believed even then, as I do now, that it was up to us still in school and at home to do our part in what was to be a great struggle. I knew I would be called on sometime in the next two years, so I started trying to determine where I might fit. The Army recruiting office in Wichita told me to wait a year and keep on with school. So next I tried the Marines and got the same answer. At that, I gave up for the time being and spent the time trying to make up for the time wasted. I played in the band and took my homework a lot more seriously.

I had worked for the Cities Service Oil Company on the pipeline "gang" the summer of 1941. It was a fill in job, but not one that one would ordinarily think of as one for a High School student. This was a man's job and a very hard one. In thinking back on it, I believe this was what was turning me from a kid into something a little more mature. The "gang" was responsible for building and maintaining the pipelines which transported the crude oil from the wells to the tanks for storage before being shipped to the various refineries. The tanks were our responsibility also.

There were a certain amount of heavy machines and tractors, to dig the ditches the pipes were buried in, but a great deal of the digging was done with shovels, picks and muscle power. The pipes themselves were sized from 6 inch to 20 inch size. These pipes were placed in the ground and then connected together. We had experienced welders who did the welding work. When it came to trying to thread two 20 inch pipes together it was again man (or boy) against two 500 pound sections of steel pipe. We used pipe tongs—in the basic shape of a pair of pinch pliers, but they were 6 feet long and weighed about 100 pounds. It took 4 men to do the work. Two men would hold one pair of tongs on one section, while another two men would turn the other sections so the screw grooves would mesh. It wasn't easy. The grown men who were permanent employees were mostly uneducated and relied more on muscle power than brain power. They gave me a hard time at first, but I stayed with it and eventually they came to accept that I was not a softy and they gave me the nickname of "Hando". Hando was the word they used to identify one that could line up the two pipes so they could be fitted together.

Cleaning out the tanks was another job I would never forget. The tanks were huge, each holding 55,000 barrels of crude oil. On each farm there were anywhere from 10 to 20 of these tanks.

Crude, by definition is not pure. It has a lot of impurities that settle to the bottom and gradually accumulate on the bottom of the tank. The name for that accumulation of stuff was called basic settlement. The men called it BS (for its equivalent profane name). To get to the BS, the tank would be emptied of the good crude oil down to about 12 inches from the bottom. 20 inches from the bottom was a door, about 36 inches square, on the side of the tank that was sealed while the Crude was in the tank.

The only way to remove the BS was for a man to take an ordinary five gallon bucket and a small shovel, crawl into the tank through that small door and scoop a bucket full and carry it back outside. The inside of the tank in the summer time was hot—anywhere from 150° degrees to *way too hot*. We were timed and could only go in one man at a time so the foreman could keep track of who was inside. The maximum time allowed was one minute. On really hot days when the afternoon sun was directly on the tank they reduced the time to 30 seconds.

If you are wondering about this seemingly unrelated tale of my trials it will be explained later when I get to the summer of 1943 in Alabama and the summer of 1944 in the swamps of Lousy Anna. One experience was not much worse than the other.

Summer of 1942 I filled in for some men who had been called up to serve in the Armed Forces. This job was much easier, but still was a man's job with a man's pay.

This was at a tank farm away from our home, so I had to room at the home of the farm manager. My job was the midnight shift at the building where the pumps were located, they received the oil from the pipeline and pumped it to the refineries. The incoming oil was stored in the big tanks before being shipped out. It was my job to "gauge" the tanks hourly because oil was continually being received. When the tank got to capacity I would shut the oil off, switch the incoming oil to another tank and record the full tank in the log book. There were often as many as 5 or 6 tank changes per shift. Between times I monitored the huge pumps and did sampling of the oil I took off the full tanks to assure that the oil had the right viscosity.

I had the responsibility of maintaining this program 6 days a week. I was basically a loner so the long nights and long weeks away from home were not a particular problem. The main problems were the two teen age daughters of the manager. They delighted in making my life miserable. The worst was when I was in the bathroom. They would come rushing in trying to catch me in an embarrassing position, which was often. There were no locks on the door.

But this was nothing compared to the lack of privacy that was waiting for me just a few short months ahead.

I tried the Navy's V-12 program. I went to Kansas City to take the tests and the physical. I passed the tests just fine and was sent to a medical facility for the physical. My eyes were 20-15, my heart was in the right place and working beautifully, and nothing was found wrong until I went to the dentist. It took him about two minutes to find that I had a serious overbite and could not easily put the upper teeth in line with the lower teeth without a strain. The verdict? I was told that I could not hold the oxygen tube in my mouth properly, and therefore could not fly the current airplanes. Furthermore, if I was on a ship and the big guns were being fired, I could not clamp down properly and the concussion would break my jaw.

Another try and another failure. This was getting frustrating.

I did not have to wait long for the solution.

Our graduation day came and we all paraded across the stage to receive our diplomas. All the parents and friends were there and afterwards we all went home. No such thing as an all night boozing and drug party with tuxedos and limos, etc.

Two days later on Monday, I received a letter in the mail. I opened it and there in great big letters was:

Chapter 3

In The Army Now

GREETINGS FROM THE PRESIDENT

I was hereby informed that I was to be drafted into the Army and was to report to Ft. Leavenworth, Kansas in 10 days. It was to be my privilege and duty to spend the duration of the War in Uniform. It went on to state that I would be receiving actual orders in a few days. When it came I had been picked to carry the orders for myself and nine other guys that were in the same boat (er boots).

I did my goodbyes to all my friends and wrote letters to my relatives telling them of the good news. And in 10 days, sure enough, I was on the railroad platform with the others and we bid farewell to home, friends, and anything else that might be familiar. So, boring was out and apprehension was in. It was a tearful scene and was repeated thousands of times the next five years.

Upon arriving in Ft. leavenworth we were met by what would become in the next few months, our worst nightmares. They all had stripes on their sleeves and mean looks on their faces. We came to learn later that this was normal. They were called non-coms. We were marched (if our shuffling could be called marching) to the barracks where we were to stay until assigned to our respective training camps.

We all learned a lot of new words, 90% of which are unprintable. We were called anything from scum to things a lot worse. We did eventually come to realize that this was the old Army way to instill discipline in the new recruits.

We were marched to the medical facility where we were lined up and walked down a line of soldiers who had been recruited because they liked to hurt things. Each one of them had a syringe filled with vile stuff that they shot into each arm and butt as we tried to hurry through. Some of the guys passed out and stayed on the concrete until they recovered and finished the immunization procedure. Those of us who could still waddle, were taken to another building for uniforms. We stripped to the buff, put our civilian clothes on the counter and took the new stuff. At first, nothing fit, but eventually we could exchange each item that did not fit for something that almost fit. Then back to the barracks to collapse on our bunks.

That did not last long either. At nine pm two non-coms walked through the barracks routing us out of a sound sleep. We were told to put a spare set of underwear, uniform shirt and pants, shoes and socks and of course our shaving gear into our clothing bag. As we sat on our foot lockers at the foot of the bed we wondered "what next?"

All too soon we were taken outside and loaded into trucks and whisked away. To where? Either no one seemed to know or they were being secretive on purpose. If we had been more experienced at that moment on the way the Army works, we would have known that we were not told on purpose.

We traveled from Ft. Leavenworth to Kansas City. We knew the rain had been falling pretty heavily for a few days and now we saw the results and where we fit in. The Missouri and the Kansas rivers were overflowing their banks. Our job for the next few days was to fill sand bags and make dikes out of them to protect water works and some other sensitive areas. We did this without hardly catching a breath or a minute of shut-eye. We were all soft and although most of us had done hard labor before, we had been in school for several months letting our muscles get flabby. It was pure torture.

Finally it was over, the water was going down and we were taken back to Ft. Leavenworth. I suppose we had performed a good service.

Next morning the non-commissioned officers took over. We were routed out at day break and told to stand by our bunks. A second lieutenant came in and made a speech about how we were now in the Army (surprise) and our lives were going to change. He admonished us to obey every command by anyone with a stripe on his sleeve and to do it immediately. He then turned around and departed. His was just the first of many speeches we sat through the next few days. But speeches were not the worst of it. Learning to march, right face, left face, about face and forward was morning till night. Everyplace we went it was in some sort of formation. We went to lectures, to Mickey Mouse movies and the most humiliating of all, to the short arm inspections. I did not realize how shy most of us were until that first experience. We were told to take off all our clothes (to the buff) and put on the raincoats we had been issued. We were then marched across the camp to the medical unit. We were lined up and went single file through a door where an Army Doctor was standing. At his side were some enlisted men we were told were medics. When it became my turn in front of the Dr. he said "Open your raincoat, skin it back and milk it down". I did not have the slightest idea what he was talking about. I stood there with a dumb look on my face and he looked back at me like I was some hick from the country. Of course he was right, but with the same tired voice he said, "take that small wiener between your legs, pull the skin back and squeeze the wiener and milk it like milking a cow". It took me a couple of seconds to perform this unique task, all to the roars of laughter from the medics, and a couple of titters from a couple of nurses that I had not noticed standing in a doorway. I passed the test (which was to see if I had any sex related diseases), buttoned my raincoat and nearly ran out the door. This little scene was to be repeated at least every month until I was dischared three years later. When we returned to our barracks we sat around and talked about this procedure and at last were able to laugh about it. It became routine. In fact so routine that we had one non-com who would be marching us to this inspection and when we passed by a group of Wacs he would give the command "open raincoats". The Wacs would applaud, the non-com would give the command "close raincoats" and we would go marching on, singing ribald ditties which everyone except me seemed to know.

In this cultural environment we learned to do a form of marching that wasn't good, but seemed to be enough for those who had been chosen to teach this skill to us.

One day we were taken to the edge of the military area and were told to sit on our keisters facing a huge block building that we learned was Leavenworth Prison. The building was on a hill about 300 yards from where we sat. In front of us was a high fence with concertino wire on top. The hill going up to the building was about a hundred yards wide. What they wanted us to see was a rock wall about 5 feet tall and the full width of the field. Prisoners were taking the rocks, one by one, and carrying them about 10 yards and making another wall. When they had completed this wall they repeated the process and carried the same rocks back to the original wall position and made the wall again. This was the work they did hour after hour, day after day.

After we watched this until it was almost dark, we were given a lecture about going AWOL (away without leave) from the Army. We were told that many of those prisoners we watched were discharged soldiers and would be doing the rock wall bit until the war was over. That night in the barracks we decided that we would do everything we could to avoid that particular task.

After a few more days of learning all these fun things we received news that we would be shipping out to our respective basic training camps. So we were rounded up and herded out like so many cattle to the train station where we were loaded on a train bound for Anniston, Alabama and the infantry training center Ft. McCellen. We were turned over to the next group which we had been assured would be 100 times worse than the past.

Chapter 4

Moving On

They were right.

    The non-coms that greeted us were many times worse than the ones we had just survived. The language was more profane, the voices shouting at us were louder, and the level of schooling they had slept through was obvious. Their language was not just terrible, it reeked of lack of knowledge of how to put two words together that made sense. It took us awhile to catch onto this new language but for our survival we had no choice. One grizzled old sergeant on that first day walked in front of our assembly and pronounced "Grab yer piller kases and fall out". In a near shout he tried for 10 minutes to explain that we were to take our pillow cases off the pillows, fill them with our dirty clothes and come back to the same spot. And on it went.

    The next day we were informed that we would be told all about sexual diseases. And sure enough, we were taken to the post theater and saw the first of what we laughingly called the Mickey Mouse movies. Most of us had never heard of the diseases they talked about and showed us. After looking at the bloody, oozing sores in and around the private parts of both males and females, most of us decided that we would never get married or look at a female again. And just so there might be someone of us that strayed, we were given condoms to carry with us when we left the base. In fact there was a condom inspection as we left the gate just to be sure we had them in our pockets. We found it strange that there was never an inspection when we returned to see if we had made use of this rubberized protection. "Oh well" we said, "it's the Army". Incidentally, this viewing of the Mickey Mouse movies was to be repeated several times during my 3 years in this bizarre world.

Part of our intro into the wonderful world of the Army was the toilets. Imagine a row of toilet bowls with seats but no tops, each one no more than 2 feet from the other. Imagine also a dozen guys sitting on those stools doing their utmost to elimate the unfamiliar mess hall chow. From there it is not hard to imagine the odor and the sounds. I really believe this was all a plot to take away our dignity and our will to do anything but what we were told. The showers were also a fun place to be. One big room lined with shower heads, no partition to let you do your scrubbing in private. The few guys that played the old Navy game of pickup the soap were given a less than honorable discharge and sent home to mama. The rest of us avoided contact at any cost. It all sounds horrible, but was routine at all Military facilities. So it was get used to it. And we did just that. Some of us adjusted our time when we used the facilities. For awhile I skipped breakfast so I could do my morning duties while most of the rest of them were eating. I had not had much breakfast at home so it was not difficult.

One of the first things we learned was that all the tests in Fort Leavenworth had a special significance. The army was looking for likely people to send to special schools for special jobs. I found that all my scouting around before being drafted paid off. At least someone was paying attention. Several of us were chosen to be included in the ASTP (Army Specialized Training Program). So we had passed the AGCT intelligence tests and the results were put in our record books. We were to go to an Infantry Training Post and then would be selected to be assigned to the specialized schools such as Medical, Legal, Construction, at selected Universities.

A lot of this information had not been given to us at Leavenworth, but we were clued in a little bit at a time. I guess they thought we might push to move on earlier than scheduled. And we just might have done that.

In the meantime we had our training to take care of. And it was a hard road. The weather in Alabama is hot and muggy in the Summer. We broke a sweat just standing in line waiting to do something. I sometimes think that a soldier spends about a third of his time standing in a line waiting for something to happen or to go someplace unpleasant. The one good thing about the early sweat was that if the wind came up just a little our fatigue uniforms served as a perfect air conditioner.

I soon found out that I was not in good shape like I thought I was. You would think that I would lose even more pounds off my slim 140 pound body, but that was not the case. Regular meals and hard work bulked me out to 200 pounds of muscle in about 6 weeks. And I was beginning to enjoy the activity, even though I griped about it just like everyone else.

Early on we were introduced to the local reincarnation of the torture chamber—it was called Bain's Gap. It really was just a hill compared to others I had seen, but this one was in Alabama and seemed to be a mile straight up and a mile straight down. In reality it was probably no more than a thousand feet in elevation. The Alabama part of it was the heat and 102% humidity.

We had to go over this hill to and from the training area. In this area there was the rifle range, the obstacle courses and other drill grounds. We spent many hours each day going through the heavy training that is necessary to turn a bunch of young guys into soldiers.

I really enjoyed the target practice. I was a little awed by the kick of the standard Garand rifle, but learned early on to keep the butt of the rifle tight against my shoulder. We all had bruises from the kick for a few days, but they soon went away. I had been using a rifle since a teenager, so I at least knew which end was the one I aimed at the target. It was funny (but a little scary) to hear the non coms up and down the line screaming at some of the soldiers to quit waving the rifles around and aim them only in one direction. Lots of them had never held a gun in their lives and had no idea how dangerous they were unless you were familiar with them.

We carried our rifles over the obstacle course. It added an additional weight to all the other packs and accessories we carried. The courses were different at the different Army bases. This one was probably one half mile long and considered difficult. And it was. The most difficult obstacle was the 12 foot high wooden fence we had to climb over. It had just a few places on the face where you could get a toe and finger hold. We learned quickly to have someone boost you to the top and then he in return would reach down to help him up and over. Another fun obstacle was the water (mud) hole. It was necessary to swing over this puddle with a rope hanging down from a tree limb. There were many other obstacles that added to the difficulty.

All of our skills did not come all at once. Each morning we would start out not knowing where we were going or what new things we would experience. Sometimes we would sit on the ground and listen to an officer or non com give a lecture on some phase of being a soldier. We learned how to conduct ourselves on base and off. We learned saluting in the little town of Anniston, Alabama. It was built on a square with sidewalks on all four sides. There was not much to do in Anniston except walk around the square. Officers and enlisted men were all doing the same thing and the chore of saluting became almost crazy. We would have to salute the same officer maybe 20 times before giving up and going to have a coke or cupa. Several of us decided that the bowling alley was where we would spend most of our time. Remembering the mickey mouse movies we avoided the many girls plying the oldest profession. They too saluted the officers but with a different type of salute, which I will not describe. Anyway we became pretty good at bowling, and saluting, and saluting, and saluting.

The hikes became commonplace. Over Bains Gap and back, 5 miles with fully loaded 60 pound packs, 10 miles with and 10 miles without, and the most fun of all (if you like blisters) the 25 mile with full pack and Garand Rifle. Lots of guys could not make it, maybe on purpose because they ended up on permanent kitchen duty which meant no future combat. The rest of us plodded on like we had good sense and the next day meant the other fun thing which was infiltration trench. 3 feet deep trenches 100 feet long were covered with barbed wire and then filled with about 6 inches of water which made the most wonderful mud. Each soldier would have to crawl the length of the ditch with live machine gun bullets going overhead just above the barbed wire. If your rifle was dirty when you got to the end of the ditch you were made to go back to the start, clean your rifle and go through the ditch again. When the last one made it through we marched back over the gap with the muddy clothes still on our backs. The showers were busy that night. What did we learn with that drill? We all agreed that it boiled down to one thing, "Keep your butt down".

Several of us decided that we would take advantage of a free bus going to Atlanta. We had heard of Peachtree Avenue and of Atlanta's claim to have the best looking girls in the USA. We started our walk at the bus terminal that was also the start of Peachtree Avenue. Going one way was about a thousand GI's from all over. Coming the other way was another thousand doing the same thing. It was just like walking around the square in Anniston, Alabama. Salute, salute, salute. Not only that, but not a pretty girl (or any other kind) was in sight. After about an hour of this and a stop for a coke, we headed back to the bus terminal and took the first bus back to camp. So much for a week-end of frolic. After that we did not even try to go out on those precious days away from training. We did go straight to the bowling alley where I worked my way up to a 188 average. Someone told me this was good.

The hikes along the back roads were an eye opener. The people in the country lived a very poor life. The houses were just shacks and the yards consisted of bare dirt which became mud after the frequent rains. The kids we saw were all barefoot and their clothes were ragged and dirty. There was no laughing and running around like most kids do, but they sat on the sagging porch or in an abandoned car. The adults we saw were not in any better shape. We later discussed how fortunate we had been in our lives.

Then there was always some kind of entertainment. Minor actors and musicians came by to put on their perfomances. Some were good, and some were not. We discovered later that some of the camps got first class shows, but there were too many of us and too few of them to go around. We would just have to wait until we were sent to more well known camps or overseas. I did find that things got much better the closer we were to the actual battlefield.

Since some of us were in the special services program, we were constantly being taken out of training and given tests. I do not believe that the standard IQ tests are valid since there is a big difference whether you have had any sleep the night before, or just returned from hard training, or if you are in a good situation and relatively happy. For instance—The first test at Ft. Leavenworth was the same afternoon we returned from 3 days and nights filling sandbags to hold back flood waters. My score was 115. Two weeks later in Alabama after a hard hike my score was 124. The third test (same content) was taken in Miami Beach and the score was 135. Then, after 6 months at the University of Buffalo in the Aviation Cadet Program when I believed I was soon to be at flight school my score was 145. Go figure!

Anyway the training continued. We kept going over Bains Gap morning and evening. In the beginning it claimed many victims who just could not handle the strain. They were mostly the smokers and those with a little too much belly fat. They literally fell by the wayside and a truck came along to pick them up. Some were taken on to the training area where they were subjected to some very profane remarks from the non coms. I learned many words I did not know existed while sitting on the sidelines and feeling sorry for those on the receiving end. Thankfully, I was able to survive that first couple of weeks by remembering the first weeks on the oil pipeline gang. It was tough going but became much easier as we went along with the routine of physically becoming in better shape and of course of gradually adding to the weight on the back packs and other equipment. It was a difficult commute every day.

The rifle range and the obstacle course were on the backside of Bains Gap. Both of these torture devices deserve a line or two.

First, the easy one. The rifle range is easy to understand as long as you keep the rifle butt hard against your shoulder. The Garand was then the rifle of choice for the infantry and served as the prime weapon for infantry all during the war.

As a preliminary there were the usual lectures. The first was the admonition that the rifle was NEVER NEVER called a gun. During these lectures we learned how to take care of the rifle. We learned how to take it apart and put it together again. First to do it slowly, then faster and faster until the final test was to disassemble and then put it together while blind folded. After we mastered this we went on to the 30mm carbine, the 45 cal. Colt pistol, the Browning Automatic Rifle (BAR). When we called it the big rifle we got a frown and chewing out by the older regular army non coms. Those non coms had a hard time with what were later on called Citizen Soldiers.

The maximum shooting distance of the rifle range was 500 yards with trenches and bunkers every 50 feet to test different distances. Most of the shooting was done from the prone position for the simple reason that is the position most used in actual combat. Later on we practiced shooting from the hip and in a standing position. The latter was for emergency reasons. I was surprised that we did not have lectures on what is considered emergencies.

We were divided into two groups—one group on the firing line and the other group in the pits manning the targets. The ones in the pits had a couple of flags on a pole—one white, the other one red. The group on the firing line would wait until they heard the starter yell "all clear on the firing line" then fire a designated number of rounds (not shots), usually 3. The guys in the pit would put a white flag over the holes in the target (WHEN) it hit the target. If the target was missed altoghether the pit crew would wave the red flag back and forth across the target. Every one up and down the firing line could see when you missed. These red flags were called "Maggie's Drawers". To the dismay of the non coms we wondered out loud what kind of girls called Maggie wore red drawers. We suggested that maybe it was time for another mickey mouse movie.

I became proficient in all the weapons and won several contests during our training. The prize was either an extra day on a pass or relief from KP duty. KP was a breeze—sitting around in the shade peeling spuds and doing dishes, sure beat 10 miles with full packs on a day when the temperature was around 110. Now, THAT'S HOT!

We could hardly wait until we had our shower and a change of clothes to rush over to the PX and put a nickel in the dispenser and get that ice cold bottle of coca cola. It may have been bad for us, but since we did not know that, we enjoyed. After the cool-off period we would sit in the day room and read the magazines that were supplied by the Red Cross and other Charities. The evening meal was in the mess hall. That was next on our agenda. Lots was written and lots of complaints were voiced by the GI's, but I enjoyed most of the things the cooks served. I must have enjoyed it because I joined this frolic at a very skinny 140 pounds and by the end of basic training I was an all muscle 200 pounds. We had good medical attention. It was sort of routine after a while to fall out for shots for things I had never heard of. The taking of blood samples happened once a month. All of this attention must have done some good because I never had so much as a cold all the time we were in serious training. One Sunday morning I woke up and could not open my mouth more than a quarter inch. I missed all three meals that day and went to the dentist the next morning. He found out that my gums were inflamed and swollen to cover my two back molars. He did his thing and I ended up with the two molars missing.

After the evening repast we usually went bowling or went to a movie. We had a few famous people come through, but not the real famous ones like Bob Hope, Harry James, etc. It was at least a break from the intense work we were engaged in, namely how to maim and kill and otherwise do all sorts of terrible, mean things to the SOB's that started this mess. Mostly we were too tired at the end of the day to do anything that required much effort. On weekends there was at least one pickup baseball or basketball game, but no one put much effort or time into it.

We lost all sense of time, one day going into the next. It could have been boring but they always seemed to come up with a new twist in our training.

One hot afternoon we were requested (read demanded) to fall out with a full pack. Full pack meant all necessary clothes, half of an army tent, sleeping bag, trenching tools (shovels), canteen and mess kit, rifle and ammunition belt (no ammunition since we were not allowed to carry same yet). I often wondered if that requirement was to keep us from shooting the non coms. When we were all assembled in front of our barracks we marched out of camp in another direction than we had used before. About a mile out of camp we came up to a small lake that was held by a dam that was about 10 feet wide. The Sergeant marched us straight across the dam until about half way. He gave the order "column left march". That meant we would step directly into the deep part of the lake with all that weight on our backs. There was a lot of backing off and shouting. I was the lead in our squad and just behind all the uproar going on ahead of us. I knew that I was a decent swimmer so I lead our squad in a column left and stepped off into the water. When I did not sink my guys followed me in the water. It was amazing but I did not need to swim. The tightly packed back packs acted like a flotation device and we floated and paddled to the closest solid land and sat back and watched the rest of the troops fight the water and their fears. Soon it was completed and we were allowed to sit in our wet clothes while an officer explained in detail that which we already knew. The walk back to our barracks was the most comfortable we had ever had. The combination of movement and the soaked clothes and pack made for a walking air conditioner. As with all other aspects of the Army, there was a down side. Our clothes were not only wet, but they were muddy and sweaty. We were rather messy also. Shortly there was a run on the showers as we tried to get ourselves clean and scrub our dirty clothes at the same time.

There was also a training of another sort. We sat for hours listening to officers show movies of Nazi's and Jap's doing bad things and lecturing us on and on about how we hated the enemy and warned us to not forget our goal.

The training was hard, but had a good purpose. The Germans and Japs were seasoned soldiers and had been building up their armies and engaging in actual warfare since the 30's. We were a soft, peaceful group of young guys that were taken out of our protected existence and were forced to become tough and aggressive as quickly as possible. Interspersed in the training there were lectures from some of the older guys that were either regular army or had been in the last of the fight in WWI. We were lectured about the skill as well as the cunning of the enemies. It was a real exercise in the necessary propaganda of war. In short we were taught to hate the Germans and Jap's. We were also taught to hate anyone who would commit treason or assist the enemy in thought or deed.

Our minds were being trained as well as our bodies.

And things were beginning to get into gear to plan for our future in the Military. Late October 1943 there appeared on the bulletin boards a list of all the different choices we would have to make. Some could sign up to be a medic, some could choose to go into the engineers to learn how to build and tear down bridges. The choice to become an officer and go to OCS (Officers candidate school). There were a lot of barracks discussions about being an Officer. That one looked the best until the notices were posted that the Air Corps (later to become the Army Airforce) needed condidates to become pilots.

About 200 signed up immediately. We were all relieved from the day to day training to take physicals and IQ tests required for acceptance. Those were the mother of all tests—just plain HARD. There was math, science, current events and everything else under the sun.

It took three full days for the tests.

200 signed up and took the tests. 25 passed the tests and were accepted. Little did we know that 12 of those that passed would go through the rest of our Military life together and remain in contact for the next 60 some years.

Chapter 5

Whoopee

SPECIAL ORDER NO. 266 DATED 9 NOVEMBER 1943 was issued transferring us to USAAFETTC NO. 4 (US ARMY AIRCORPS EMERGENCY TECHNICAL TRAINING CENTER) at Miami Beach, Florida.

Things were definitely looking up.

Orders were written up and we were transferred to a new way of living. I suppose you could say that we were given a quit claim deed to leave one service and change our insignia to another.

Twelve test weary guys in a state of limbo. We were not recruits and soldiers, nor were we Cadets and so it seemed we sort of floated around for a week or so. The first order was to travel by train to Atlanta and transfer to another train to Miami Beach clear at the bottom of Florida. We were met at the train and taken to a huge hotel that was headquarters for the Air Corps. There we met with several other groups from different Basic training centers. We went through the usual long lines to get us sorted out. First they put us in several small residential hotels. The 12 from Ft. McClellan were put in one called THE CRESCENT. It was elegant and in peace time housed summer guests (later called snow birds) mostly from New York. Some of the hotels still had some of these guests—elderly men and women who did nothing but sit on the porches and take in the sun. Most of them looked like red prunes.

We thought we were through with tests, but we were wrong. The Air Corps had to decide where each person would go—to be a cadet and learn to fly, or be sent to other areas to be air crew, or be sent to someplace else to be ground crew.

The training was certainly laid back compared to basic infantry. They had us march to another big hotel for our meals, and had us play sports or swim in the ocean. It felt like they wanted us to stay in shape, but make it seem light.

I met the first celebrity I had ever seen one day on one of the side streets where about 8 of us were walking on the way to the beach. The officers lived in individual houses so they would not be contaminated by the enlisted.

We were on one side of the street on a sidewalk and coming toward us about a block away was a lone officer. We automatically checked our ties and pants and shirt creases because we had been chewed out many times in Alabama. Suddenly out of an alley came 5 or 6 civilian young men and they all jumped on the Officer, pushing him to the ground. One of our guys said "We can't let them get away with that". It was not much of a battle. Any one of them by himself would run for cover. The fight was short and we left them on the ground and told the Officer to keep on going and we attempted to do the same, but there had been several witnesses, and since we were in Officer territory, we were asked (ordered) to stay. We thought that the least we could expect was to be sent back to Alabama.

It was quite a shock to have several Captains and Majors shake our hands one by one. The Officer who had been down had handled himself pretty well once he got up from being blind sighted. Guess he had learned a few tricks during his movie days. After all Clark Gable should have been able to handle those punks without our help.

The MP's rounded up (had to pick up some of them) and carted them away. We took some ribbing over the incident.

The weather was warm and we took advantage of some tours offered by some of the service organizations. The USO was always around doing a wonderful job of keeping our thoughts away from our future lives. We went to Cypress Gardens and did some water skiing, and there was always a first run movie.

The latest round of tests were favorable for the 12 guys that were hanging together and we found that we were selected for the College training in preparation for eventually becoming pilots, navigators or bombadiers.

Something else to get used to. In the Infantry we were addressed as "You *^%^(*#@ poor excuse of a soldier". Then at Miami Beach we were addressed by our last name with a Mr. in front of it, (as in Mr. Leek). Soon we would be Cadets and later on it would be Officers (sir).

On December 11, 1943 we boarded a train to be delivered to the University of Buffalo, New York. Because of the war and the need to transport war materials as well as military people every old train engine and passenger car was brought out for service. Most of the windows would not work, the seats were wooden benches, there was no facility for food or water. We prepared for a long miserable trip North where the weather was reported near zero. The temperature in Miami Beach was 80 degrees.

We slept in our seats or on the floor. Our so-called meals were prepared in a make shift kitchen in a baggage car in the middle of the train. At meal times we would form another line to pick up our food on a tray and carry it to our seats or squat on the floor. The train moved at a snail's pace. Probably it was because the operators thought it would fall apart if they went to fast. It was interesting to watch out the widows (dirty) and see the landscape slowly go from green grass and shrubs to leafless trees and brown grass. The clothing on the people we saw changed also—from shorts and light shirts to long pants, shirts and jackets, and finally to boots and heavy coats. What did not change was the attitude of the people watching us as we went by or at the various stops along the way. It soon became clear that we would not have to eat the food on board, because of the many women and young girls with trays of sandwiches, cookies, cake and soft drinks they offered us. It was a heartfelt thought that was more than appreciated by every one of us. By the time we reached Buffalo on December 13 we could not eat another bite.

Chapter 6

Finally Delivered to Buffalo

When we were finally delivered to Buffalo we were met by an Officer and two non coms who had busses waiting for us. It was snowing and cold and we had no warm clothes. That was taken care of as soon as we reached the University of Buffalo. We were taken to the supply room and issued all new clothes. Warm clothes. After that we were assigned living quarters in the dormitories on campus. These accommodations were nothing like either Alabama or Miami Beach. There were 4 men to a room. We each had our own closet, a regular bed and space around that bed to call our own. The latrines were modern and the stools had stalls around them, and there were enough shower heads that we only had to share with 4 or 5 instead of two or three dozen. We took our meals in the cafeteria, which had been redone to make it a little more like military, but still a cut above anything we had seen yet.

We got down to business in short order. The first order was to be assigned our schedule of classes. Mainly we were to study mathematics and its relationship to flying, physics, also geography which would get us back home after swarming all over the enemy. English language so we could speak to each other (this had little to do with the language spoken by the Brits), meteorolgy and military science. The subject that intrigued us the most was that class we attended every day called HOW TO BECOME AN OFFICER AND A GENTLEMAN. Here was where we learned the Army understanding of the concept. We were given instructions on how to sit and eat properly. We studied how to hold our own in a conversation with anyone. We learned the rules on how to treat each other and how to treat the enlisted men.

The rules and regulations concerning the Army were thoroughly discussed. Then there were sessions on proper respect for the Flag, when and where to wear your hat (as well as the rest of the uniform) and when and where and who we should salute. They were very deep and serious subjects and we were not allowed to make fun of any of it.

The studies were tough and required a lot of home work.

The physical training was extremely rigorous. Every week day morning, before breakfast, we fell out in the parking lot regardless of the weather and in our shorts, tee shirts and tennis shoes (the regular shoe size) we ran a 5 mile route through the streets and back to the campus. Most of the time it was snowing and below freezing. If we did not do it properly, or slowed to a walk enroute, the penalty was 5 laps around the parking lot. When the snow was deep and the running hard, the day could start out pretty terrible.

Inside the gym the "must attain" goal was 100 push ups, 100 sit ups, and 100 pull ups. We all attained that goal before the end of our stay in Buffalo. In between all these activities we played basketball, volleyball and tennis (all of these indoors). The most serious was the basketball. We played games with several of the small colleges close by. We even took the time to learn the Queen Ann Rifle Drill. This was the fancy things you sometimes see in the movies. It is basically for showing off. It's sort of like a dance step—you twirl the rifle, go thru the port and present arms, all the time doing the steps in a rythym, while a leader calls out the cadence. Fun stuff but did not mean a whole lot as far as training went.

So much for the physical stuff. What I was really interested in was the dance band. I called Dad at home and asked him to send my trombone. Surprise-surprise, even with all the problems with movement of personal property the trombone arrived in about 4 days. Five of the guys that had come this far also had instruments. With all of the activity we managed to practice every week day evening. We may have been worn out from studies and physical activities, but playing those Big Band songs took all the fatigue away.

Radio station WBEN asked us to play every other week. What we did not know at the beginning was that they had arranged for the big names in the music business to bring some of their side men to join us. We were fortunate to have Tommy Dorsey, Ray Anthony, Harry James and several others to play alongside us. My greatest thrill was when I played my solo on American Patrol. Tommy Dorsey stood alongside me and played the second part. I was in such a state I almost couldn't get started, but we got caught up in the music and it was agreed that we sounded fabulous. ***My 15 minutes of fame!!!!!!!***

Our every other week gig was broadcast over a small network of NBC stations in about 6 cities in New York State. We also played for a couple of parades, three concerts at Kleinhans Music Hall, one concert in Shea's Hippodrone and for our own Detachment dances.

The city of Buffalo made off-duty social life very enjoyable. Admission was free at most theaters, transportation facilities were free to anyone in uniform. Very seldom did we have to pay for our meals in hotels or restaurants. It was easy to get into town. All we had to do was walk out the front entrance of our dormitory and stand at the curb heading towards town. Always someone would stop and give us a ride even if it took them out of their way. Generally, we found the people of Buffalo to be friendly and generous.

So, this is a good time to talk a little about Buffalo. When I said it was snowy, windy and cold most of the time, I was not kidding. That has to be the coldest place I had ever been up to that time.

Buffalo is located between Lake Erie and Lake Ontario. Niagra Falls is the drop off from one lake to the other. When it is rainy and windy the spray from the falls drifts around and causes the humidity to reach 100%. It is just like a drizzle that won't stop. Whatever we did outside we were either wet or cold-or both.

We had just about settled in and were concentrating on our classes and other military duties when we realized that it would soon be Christmas. For many of us this would be the first Christmas away from home. We spent some time with letters and calls home as well as asking our parents to include our new address in their Christmas cards.

In the main hall there was a giant bulletin board used mostly for social occasions and special activities that were not on the regular schedule. There were a couple of write-ups in the local papers about the new group of future airmen in town. Suddenly, about a week before Christmas the bulletin board was completely covered with notices of families that wanted to host an airman for Christmas dinner. There were so many requests it was hard to know which one to pick. Some guys did not want to attend any of them, but most of us thought it was a wonderful idea.

Several of the guys that had started out together at Ft. McClellan were becoming more acquainted. Jim Hentges and I stood in front of the bulletin board and made a choice based on the fact that one family wanted two guys and lived in Ontario Canada. We called them and made arrangements to arrive at 10 am on the Sunday before Christmas Day. We had made a good choice.

We took a bus to Niagra Falls and Mr. and Mrs. Kennedy picked us up there and took us to their home. Before we even reached their house you would have thought we were their own sons. When we arrived at their home we found out that they had two daughters that were near our age—one was 17 and the other was 19. We had a wonderful traditional dinner and enjoyed the feeling that we were family. The girls said they were glad we could join them. Jim Hentges made the remark later that it was too bad that they treated us like BROTHERS. It was a very special day for two young soldiers away from home. We kept in touch to let them know how much we enjoyed that day. In a letter home I told the folks about that day and later I was told in a letter from the Kennedy's that my mother wrote to them thanking them for taking care of us.

The Kennedy's drove us back to Niagara Falls. Before taking the bus back to our current home away from home, we visited the museum which featured all the vehicles people had used to take themselves over the falls. Most of them did not make it. We took the "*MAID OF THE MIST*" excursion boat that took tourists below the falls and up close and much too personal. It was thunderously noisy and very wet.

Every one at the detachment was very vocal about the wonderful people they had met and the fabulous meals they enjoyed. Although the first group of invitations was around a holiday, the bulletin board was full for the rest of the time we were there. There were a couple of columns in the paper about the lavish display of "thanks to the troops", no doubt inspiring others to get in on the "Keeping up with the Jones". That last comment is probably not fair because EVERY person we came in contact with was generous and friendly. Of course there were a few who thought we were going to ravish the whole population of their daughters. Then to be absolutely honest, there were several of the cadets that were completely convinced that they were God's gift to all females.

This brings us to my very first real girlfriend.

The first Saturday after January 1, 1944, Jim Hentges and I were sitting around bored stiff. Our homework for our classes was done so we decided that instead of partaking of the exquisite food in the mess hall, we would go across the street to the sandwich shop and ice cream parlor. The selection would be better than staying inside. The place was pretty crowded with cadets that had the same thought. After we picked up our sandwiches we looked around for a place to sit. We spied two guys that were at a table for four. As we wound our way around the filled tables heading for those two empty seats we came around another table with the same situation—but what a difference. One was a tall, striking girl with long coal black hair. The other one was a blonde, and in my limited experience a real knock out. They both smiled and pointing to the two empty chairs across from them invited us to join them. We exchanged names and for the next few minutes I could not say a word. It dawned on me that I did not know how to make small talk. But it turned out that the two of them knew how—in spades. During the conversation they explained that they attended an educational institution called "Garland School for Girls" located in Boston. Talk about out of our depth!!! Surprisingly it went along much better than I thought.

The black haired one introduced herself as Franny. Her Dad, as we learned later, manufactured airplane engines and was by his own admission, making a living selling them to the military. He was a nice man and later on we were at his house frequently. Franny's Mother was a very sophisticated lady and did not look much older than Franny.

The blonde was Priscilla. Her Dad owned a factory, and a square block of downtown on which sat the Downtown Athletic Club, a club for the rich and famous. He too was a nice guy.

Both the Dad's were friendly with Jim and I and never acted as if they would rather their girls went with someone other than a soldier. Perhaps because we would soon be officers made a difference. Pricilla's Mother was not the sophisticated type. She was down to earth and gave a kiss on the cheek every time I came to visit.

Back to the meeting. We talked till late afternoon when they had to take a bus back to their homes just a block off the bus route. We agreed that we would go to Priscilla's home the next day then go to a movie. Somehow we had paired off, Jim H and Franny and Jim L and Priscilla.

Mostly we used the bus system to get around. Rarely did we have to wait more than 10 minutes for one to come by.

Gas was almost non existent, but we did use Priscilla's brother's car when we could get a coupon. The war effort was in full swing and every one was on board doing everything to conserve energy so the troops could have every resource for their fight. Priscilla's father was able to get gas once in awhile, but we never questioned him about his sources.

Another good friend, Bud Kebbekus joined us from time to time and Franny found a girl for him. Her name was Betty and looked enough like Franny that we kidded them about being sisters. They seemed to have a different agenda and only joined in with us on rare occasions.

Priscilla's brother was on a Navy Destroyer. He was older than she and had been in the Navy for a couple of years. I never met him or heard about him after we left Buffalo. She had a younger sister named Barbara who was of course still living at home.

One of the trips we took in the car was to Niagara Falls and on over to the North side of the Lake which was Canada. Priscilla's family had what they called The Farm there, where they raised race horses. The farm house was about 6 times the size of our home back in Kansas. The stables were only about 4 times the size. Everyone insisted that we ride. EVERYONE DID YOU KNOW. Since we were from Kansas and Oklahoma they figured we had been raised on horses. It was mostly true with Jim H. He was raised on a farm. It was not so with Jim L. The only horse I had ever been on was a plow horse owned by our friends in Missouri. My friend and I rode the horse bareback to his grandmothers house a half mile away. That was my total experience on horseback. I tried to get out of it by saying I could not ride without a Western saddle. The English saddles were just a flat piece of leather with high stirrups. To my amazement they produced two beautiful Western saddles, dusty but never much used. I had seen enough western movies that I knew the basics, so off we went. Those horses were bred to run and they loved their job. The place they used to run the horses was on the beach, long and sandy.

The girls challenged us to a race. I was convinced that I would end up in the water digging sand out of my ears. We trotted down the beach to a small dock and turned around. The girls said "last one to the pier (at their farm) has to do the dishes tonight". And off we went. It wasn't pretty but I bent over that saddle and gave the horse a nudge and he really took off. The girls were great riders, but got to laughing so hard at our antics they neglected to pay attention and we beat them both by a length. Jim and I were looking forward to teasing the girls about doing the dishes. We were surprised that evening when the cooking, washing and drying and clean up was done by the caretakers who lived on the farm and took care of those chores. So much for living in the fast lane. With a short stop at the falls we headed back to the U of B and the reason we were here.

And so it went every weekend and during the week whenever there was a dance or special event that the girls could attend as our dates. It was a chore keeping the cadets from running off with the girls. Those self proclaimed "ladies men" did everything they could think of to get noticed and secure a date. It bothered Jim and I at first, but as we watched how smoothly the girls handled themselves, we could sit back and watch those guys get let down, some gently, some with a thud. WE were the ones that took them home.

I cannot recall if we were told the backgrounds of the professors at the Learning Center. The location was at a university and there were some civilian classes going on. With a name like ours which was 23rd COLLEGE

TRAINING DETACHMENT each professor must have been from that level. Each one was outstanding.

Our English professor spent a lot of time on compositions and grammar. There were those that still used a lot of "young guys" or "dem dere" so he had a lot to do to bring us up to par. We called it his secret weapon. It was called HYPNOTISM. It was a legitimate weapon because there were many studies being made to develop any advantage we could develop to fight the enemy. Mr. Patrick told us of experiments to hypnotize during operations and amputations when regular anesthetics are not available. He told us of his own experience when he had a bad toothache and could not see a dentist until next day. He had a friend hypnotize him and tell him his tooth did not hurt. The tooth did not hurt until he was in the dentist's chair the following day.

There were some (most) cadets that still did not believe him so he gave us a practical demonstration. He said he would try to put the entire class to sleep. First, Mr. Patrick had the class pick out a light in the room to stare at. He then started talking in a normal tone of voice, but gradually lowering his voice to soft, gentle words that would almost talk a person to sleep even if they gave no attention to what was actually being said. He told his "guinea pigs" that they were getting sleepy and to close their eyes. He then suggested that their left arm was so weak that they could not move it, but their right arm was very strong. Next he told them to lift their right arm over their head. Three of the cadets were sound asleep with their right arms reaching up over their heads. They stayed that way while he told them that their left leg would feel no pain. We really paid close attention "those that were still awake" to what happened next. He took three long needles from his desk and pushed one into each left leg. There was not a quiver from either one of the three guys. They were sound asleep and feeling no pain that could be seen. One of the guys with a pin in his leg was told that as he left the room at close of class he would shout "oh-ho-ho". Patrick told the three men to wake up at the count of 10 and all three woke up at the same time. They were surprised at the pins in their legs. They said they felt no pain. What was surprising was that they felt no pain as they pulled the pins out.

Mr. Patrick explained that with a little more time about half the class of 26 would have been put to sleep. At this point in their studies the average was about 50%.

There were some light hearted discussions about what we had seen. One question was "could hypnosis be used on some of the beautiful young Buffalo Girls". The answer was, it was impossible to make any person go against their moral standards. A huge sigh of regret followed that answer.

It was decided and discussed that if we had a toothache or want to quit smoking we should go see Mr. Patrick. In our discussions in the evening we decided that the above might not be a good idea.

As we marched out of the classroom, the designated shouter came through with a loud OH-HO-HO! The look on his face was priceless.

Little did we know that there were lots of secret programs going on around the world. Little things like the communication problem of secure codes—the best of which was the Navajo Indians using their own language which the enemy never broke, and slightly bigger things like the atomic bomb.

We happened to be in a good spot to see first hand one of the developments. That was the helicopter. Bell had built and was testing the Air Cobra. We could not get near the plant just North of Buffalo but we could watch those tiny machines seeming to float around as they went through their tests. This development was known by most people in Buffalo, but the newspapers and radio stations did not report or acknowledge the presence of the choppers. Today's newspapers would have headlines and pictures and plans so the enemy could have easy knowledge of what we were doing.

We were asked by the Army authorities to not discuss outside the classroom, anything we talked about. It was just another way to keep someone from putting things together and gain knowledge of our plans and techniques where the air war was concerned. We were not being paranoid. Shortly after Christmas the Military Police and local Police raided a house not far from the University grounds. There was nothing in the papers or on radio even though it was obvious to bystanders that it was an important bust. When we asked about it we were told that two men had been found with information they were not supposed to have and a civilian student had been questioned. We were advised to forget the whole thing.

All of the Professors were quite vocal in their discussions about being flag waving and patriotic. The class that we liked best was the one on techniques of flying and what made an airplane stay aloft despite the laws of gravity. We studied the various types of airplanes currently in combat. One of the questions on a mid term test asked our preference when we left here. My answer was the P38—a two engine fighter with counter rotating props and two machine guns synchronized to fire between the rotations of the props. Most of the fighter planes were so small that a person 6 feet tall could not fit in the small place provided. Because the P38 did not have engines as part of the fuselage a little more room could be provided for the pilot.

I was still a little reluctant to think we would all get what we wanted but I did not worry about it too much. For a couple of the really big guys the problem was solved. They would go to the post that trained for the big bombers.

We were getting closer to graduation time and you could feel the intensity gathering steam. We spent more and more time on our homework, but we had to leave time for the social side of our experience.

All along we spent our precious free time dating our girl friends. It was surprising how many of the cadets had found a friend to share their time with. Jim H and I still double dated Franny and Priscilla. We went to the movies and to the detachment functions such as dances and sharing our mess hall whenever the cook felt like it. Both of our girls declared that the food was just OK. We would have put it a little lower than that, but the cook had gone all out when guests were to be there. The band played at several functions put on by the city of Buffalo. The girls went with us. It was on one of these outings that I found out I was deathly allergic to shell fish.

The day started off when Priscilla's Dad called me and asked if I would like to go to the Tommy Dorsey dance that night at one of the big hotels in town. He assumed that I would take Priscilla with me. When I told him that I certainly would, he said that he and Priscilla's Mom would take us to dinner before the dance. Wearing a uniform makes it easy to decide which tux I would wear. The quick notice was no problem at all.

I arrived at their house 10 minutes before the departure time. Priscilla and her Mother wore long off the shoulder dresses (pardon me-gowns). The ride downtown was in a mini limo—it was so much easier than trying to find a parking place.

The hotel dining room was magnificent. A sea of white table cloths and gleaming silver. They apologized that the waiters were all women because the men were off to war.

Each table was set with a fancy folded napkin and a tall stemmed glass with shrimp all around the rim of the glass. I asked and was told that this was a shrimp cocktail. They could not believe that I had never tasted (or seen) one before. I followed their direction and nibbled gently, carefully extending my pinky. Dinner went along OK and everything tasted wonderful.

We said goodbye to the parents and went into the ballroom where Dorsey was playing the first tune. About halfway through the third one featuring one of Dorsey's trombone solos I stumbled but caught myself. When we sat down I started feeling woozy. In just a few minutes I told Priscilla that I was sick to my stomach and had to go to the restroom.

And that is all I remembered until 3 days later.

I barely made it to the restroom where they say I heaved up everything and passed out. Priscilla asked someone to check on me. At that point one of the cadets made a pass at Priscilla and told her I was drunk and deserved to be left in the toilet. A month later he still had a scratch on his face.

A hotel person helped me up and out where Priscilla had called a cab. There was a great TO DO while they loaded me in the cab and took me to her home.

We almost beat her Parents home. He called a Doctor who stayed with me until they were sure I was going to be OK. They also called the Detachment to tell them what had happened and that I had not gone AWOL. The detachment Dr. came to their house to verify my condition.

I came to on the second day and they told me all the stuff that happened and the Doctors decided that I was allergic to shell fish and it would be wise to avoid it in the future. Several years later by mistake I ate some in a salad (they told me it was tuna). And a couple of times later I had almost the same results. It turned out that I could eat non-shell fish, but it all tasted like cod liver oil, so I just passed it all up.

One of the biggest events outside the Military stuff we were doing was the Graduation Ball a couple of weeks before going on to our next assignment. It was held at Kleinhans Music Hall and included dinner and dancing—all in formal attire. As usual our uniforms were classed as formal, so once again it was a shave, shower and shampoo and jump into the uniform. I was invited to have a snack (her folks did not drink hard stuff and neither did I) before going to the Music Hall. I had arranged for a taxi to come to their home at 7:45 so we could be on time. I had told Priscilla of the taxi ahead of time and she must have told her Dad. He had cancelled the taxi and told me that a private car would pick us up and bring us home.

Right on the dot a block long (or so it seemed) limo pulled up in front. You can imagine the attention we received when we rolled up in that. Priscilla had a new gown and looked smashing, so between the limo and my date I probably looked pretty drab.

Everyone had a wonderful time. A local dance band played all the favorites of the 40's and we danced until well after midnight. We had the limo driver take Jim H. and Franny by her residence and then Priscilla's. The driver had been instructed to then take Jim and I back to the University. What a night! We both regretted that this type of living would soon come to a close.

The 23rd College Training Detachment, University of Buffalo published a newspaper every other week with news of what was going on and tidbits about the cadets. In Volume I, No. 7 there was an item about Squadron B that read, "Jim Leek likes Buffalo. Millionaire's daughters don't grow on trees, but watch your step chum; taxes are on the way up. Besides a marriage license has a luxury tax on it".

Priscilla and I became pretty fond of each other and talk was starting to come around to the future. Nothing specific, but just what we thought we wanted out of life, etc.

Our differences soon became apparent. My wants and thoughts were pretty simple. She wanted the usual things people who have never had to think about money want. A big house, 12 kids, some traveling and college. The 12 kids was my first warning. Later on came the second warning—one I could not have guessed in a thousand years.

We were sitting around the dinner table at their house. Not much was said during the regular meal, but at dessert time—her Dad leaned back in his chair and asked "have you guys started having sex yet"? Talk about shocked. My family could not even say the word one on one, let alone with the whole family at dinner. Her sister Barbara, who was about 12 or 13, piped up and said. "Jim's going overseas and they ought to be thinking about it." That really blew my mind. I took a deep breath and looked her dad in the eye and said, "we discussed it and decided that it would not be a good idea. Things are too uncertain and I believe Priscilla should be able to meet people and feel free to follow her own lead. We will discuss it again when the War is over." There was dead silence. Mrs. was in tears and Mr. got up quickly and left the table, giving me a pat on the back as he passed by.

A few days later her Dad and I were by ourselves while we waited for the others to get home. He said that he was glad about the sex, but he did wish I would think about tying Priscilla up as a steadying influence. He then told me he would see to it that I went to college at Cornell and would put me in the meter factory with a fast climb to running it. That was the third big warning. My life would be controlled forever. Not that it would not be a good life, but I was just hard headed enough to believe I should at least try to make it on my own. And besides, how did I know that I would like running a meter factory?

Anyway, we left it at that. We spent a lot of time together and with Jim and Franny.

The training also went on and the last thing we did was take flying lessons. The routine was 10 hours in a piper cub and with no solo. That would be taken care of when we were in regular flight training.

The first hour was one that I thought would be my last. The instructor gave me a briefing about seat belts and to watch everything he did, as well as watch the horizon, the instruments, the sky etc. etc. I did not tell him that this was my first time in an airplane. Maybe I should have, but it also probably would not have helped.

We took off from the Buffalo Muni Airport and headed up towards the falls. He very slowly started to climb, going in huge circles to give me the lay of the land. He was a good tour guide as well as a good pilot. I never knew our altitude but he kicked one wing over and pulled the stick back. We rolled over and went straight down like a corkscrew. My first thought was that we had been hit by something. The next thought was that the thing lost a wing. The next thought was that I would wring his neck when we landed. He had glanced back at me and I briefly saw a smile on his face. It was then I knew I was being tested—and found wanting. My stomach gave up the struggle and eliminated the breakfast all over me, the back seat and floor.

After he leveled off he told me to take the stick and keep it straight and level using the stick and foot pedals, and the throttle which was on the side of the cockpit. I managed fairly well considering the shape I was in. When we landed I did not say a word, but went in the hangar and found some water and rags and cleaned up the mess I had made. He did not say anything to me either. I really thought I was through with flight training. One short glorious mess of a flight.

The next day we got in the plane and he said, "Take it off". We had had enough ground training at the college that I knew how it should be done, so I revved it up, went down the runway more or less in a straight line and then when it got to the speed for takeoff I pulled back on the stick and we were air borne. After that things went smoothly. I had a little trouble at first knowing whether we were going north or East, but by the 5th lesson I was going pretty well. I flew smoothly, did not try to get fancy and did nothing stupid.

We were not to have a solo flight after the 10th flight, and my log book does not record one, but we went to a little used field outside of town where we usually did our touch and go's and landed. He got out of the cockpit and said "take it up, fly one big circle and come back and land", and he walked away. It was illegal, but I made a smooth circle and a safe landing and can tell myself, if not anyone else, I soloed.

So, here we were, happy as clams, doing what we had wanted to do all along. We sang cadence songs as we marched. We did our five miles each morning, rain, snow, ice or sleet. We played basketball during the day after classes, played in the band in the evening, did our quota of 100 exercises every day, studied hard and even had time for recreation on week-ends. We watched the skies a lot because close by was an experimental installation where they were testing the new jet propelled fighter planes and the even more exotic helicopters. They flew over every day. We even had dreams about being able to eventually fly them.

The time of finals, which we all passed with flying colors, came and then the day when we all lined up on the parade ground to receive our orders to report to pre-flight. We already knew where we were to be sent and to do what. I was scheduled for P-38 training because of my height. Its cockpit was the only one where anyone over 6 ft. could be reasonably squeezed.

Chapter 7

The Dream Is Over

The first words after a long silence from the Major in charge of our detachment were that our orders had been changed. Then he proceeded to read SPECIAL ORDER NO. 2, DATED 3 MAY 1944 from General H.H. "HAP" Arnold transferring 122 Aviation Cadets from duty at AAF Base Unit to the 78th Infantry Division at Camp Pickett, Virginia.

Our dream was shattered. Most of the guys cried. I just sat on the ground with my head in my arms and tried to pull myself together. The shock was almost unbearable. Thankfully, we were dismissed and we all gathered in groups to talk it out.

A bunch of us immediately checked on all available ways we could at least get into something where we could use our recently acquired education. Tests were being given for the Coast Guard Academy. All of us had scores in the 145 range. But when we made the official application it was discovered that all slots had been filled. Next we tried the OCS which we had passed up before, but that too was filled.

The jig was up. We were doomed. All that we had worked so hard for had gone up in a puff of smoke. All those words of praise by Hap Arnold and also those Officers who were in charge of our detachment could not ease the pain.

The Army was the Army and we had no choice. The war effort was gathering momentum for the D Day invasion and warm bodies were needed.

This May of gloom and doom needed one more farewell to make our departure complete.

The night before we were to take the train to Virginia I made the journey to Priscilla's home to say goodbye. It was a pretty sad scene. We had not resolved our situation and it had to be done before I left. Her folks were with us for a part of the evening. Dinner was teary because I really believe they thought I would one day become part of their family. I told them frankly that I probably would not be able to provide for Priscilla in the way she was accustomed. I was no doubt selling myself short, but I was not particularly happy with the way they wanted to direct our lives.

Later on, Priscilla and I were sitting on the couch talking the thing out. She was in tears and I was too. It was getting late and I had to get back to the University. There was a knock on the door and she went to see who it was at this time of night. She let out a small scream and I went to see what the problem was. The problem was a tall, good looking Navy man. Priscilla was beside herself with embarrassment. It seems that this sailor was her old boyfriend who thought he was the only one. We shook hands and started talking about the military. I wondered if she wanted us to fight over her. We read that in her face and made a grand effort to pretend we were great buddies. I left before he did so my departure was a chaste kiss on the cheek. His name was Paul and his family was as rich as Priscilla's. Both families had oodles of money and it was my opinion that he was better suited to the fast lane than I was. As I left I thought to myself, "I may have made a big mistake in giving up the College Education and a secure future, but I was determined to try to make it on my own.

As it turned out, I made the best decision of my life. A year or so later I met Dee Dee Davis and except for a random thought of how my life would have been, I never looked back. I had saved the best for the last. And at this writing, the best has lasted for nearly 60 years of love and happiness.

I saw Priscilla one more time in 1945. She came to the hospital in Boston where I was being processed for my injuries. She married Paul. I returned to Kansas. We departed friends.

We are in the Infantry Now

Again

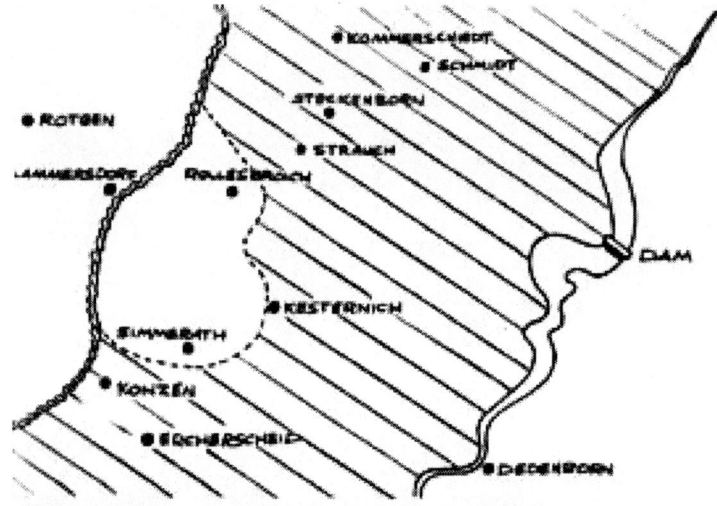

The order that kicked us out of the Air Force was dated May 3, 1944. We arrived at Camp Pickett, Virginia on May 10. The Army wasted no time in getting us out of Buffalo. Probably did not want us to sit around thinking about what had just happened.

Camp Pickett was the home base for the 78th Infantry Replacement Division. It had been originally set up as a place to train soldiers as replacements for the depleted ranks of Divisions already in Europe and the Pacific. The last big batch of replacements had just been sent to Europe to fill out the units getting in place for the invasion.

We were to be the first group to be in a full fledged combat-ready Division. Stephen Ambrose called these soldiers "Citizen Soldiers". Almost all of the new 78th recruits came from Aviation Cadets, ASTP, and other branches which had enough manpower already, or sacrificed to put troops in needed training for what was going to be a huge ground effort.

It did not take us long to realize the full extent of what had happened to us. As the escort from the Air Force turned us over to the Infantry non coms, they saluted us and said "Gentlemen, thank you for choosing the Air Force. We are sorry to see you leave. Good luck". The Air Force men then took their leave and returned to Buffalo to Deactivate the Buffalo Detachment.

The Infantry non coms lined us up and the First Class Sergeant stood in front of the group and greeted us thusly—"You God damned sissies are ours now and we are going to make sure your asses drag all the way to Berlin". The IQ level just dropped to close to 0.

It didn't take long for this group to learn the way of this advanced training. We had learned in basic how to use the weapons of war. And it did not take a mental giant to say Yes Sir and No Sir and to follow orders without question.

Physically, we from Buffalo were far ahead of those who had spent their time in classrooms and other non-physical pursuits. Those 5 mile runs every morning, and the other physical goals made us in top notch shape and we decided to not let the bad language get us down.

Probably the most demanding activity was the 25 mile forced march with full 60 pound packs. In combat a soldier must carry most of his needs with him as backup supplies were often far behind.

The next few days were spent resting our sorry butts on the ground in the hot sunshine. We were there to listen to almost the same stories we had heard in Alabama, about the infantry and its contributions to the war effort. They had no need to think we did not already know about the part played by the ground war. It was just that we would have rather been flying. We also heard the old story about sexual diseases and saw the same Mickey Mouse films. It was easy to fall asleep in the heat and the repetition of subjects we already had heard many times.

During this time we were divided into the specific units which we would be part of from that moment on.

I was assigned to M company, 309th battalion, 78th infantry division. This was called a heavy weapons company with 81mm mortars and 51mm machine guns as our weapons.

We now had our own pecking order. Privates, Privates First Class (PFC), Corporal, Sergeants and a 2nd Lieutenant. It was essential that we get to know each other and learn how things were done with our weapons.

Right off the bat the entire Battalion was put on notice that there would be a 15 mile forced march the very first weekend we were there. Full packs would be carried. Rifles instead of mortars. As an added twist, since this would be a test, the first 10 guys back to the starting point would get a full day pass in addition to the next weekend.

The route had been marked by thousands of guys who had been here before us, so there would be no cutting corners.

Off we went, already sweating with the heat.

There were 5 ex-cadets in our company and 4 or 5 in L Company. We got together the night before the march and made an agreement to help each other so we would come in near the lead to force the cadre to show us a little more respect.

The route was dusty and there were a lot of ups and downs. When we saw one of our guys falter or slow up we would work our way behind him and lift his pack until he got his breath back again. About half way one of our guys started to sing the Air Corps song "off we go into the wild blue yonder". That did not go over very well but they could not single out anyone singer so let it go.

To make it short, 10 of the ex cadets finished in the top 15. Five of us lined up shoulder to shoulder and came in at a trot and first by two hundred yards.

There would be more long hikes, forced marches and hours and hours of weapons drills. All of this was a repetition of the stuff we did in Alabama, but more intensive.

Another thing we learned was that the soldiers made great cheap labor just like the flood in Topeka and Kansas City.

During mid May, the city of Philadelphia had a strike on their hands that tied up the transportation system of busses, street cars, trucks and about anything that transported people to their jobs and goods to support the war effort. The violence was getting out of hand and needed a firm hand. The 309th was sent up to take care of this problem. We pitched tents in Fairmont Park in a driving rain. The only modern convenience was the toilets set up at one end of the Park. We did have running water. It came from the sky and ran right through our tents and collected in small lakes all over the Park.

Our job was to ride the street cars and busses WITH LIVE AMMUNITION AND FIXED BAYONETS. Our orders were short and to the point. "No one would be allowed to take over the unit or interfere with the roads, electrical overheads or do any damage to the operators who were mostly management." Thankfully a word and lowering a rifle off the shoulder kept most of the strikers at bay. There were a couple of scuffles but I was never involved in any direct contact with the strikers.

There were some good things about our duties. Almost every person who boarded the bus or street car would bring goodies for the soldiers. We always had a pocket full of cookies, apples, sandwiches, etc. It was not unusual late at night to find a soldier and one of Philadelphia's more adventurous daughters in the dark back end of the street car. The long routes into the suburbs took an hour or two to make the round trip with no other passengers on board except one adventurous daughter, a driver, one adventurous soldier and one non-adventurous soldier with rifle and bayonet braced to repulse any boarding strikers.

We were there 2 weeks and were able to take in some of the sights that were not under lock and key because of the war. The Liberty Bell was one of the historical items—along with some of the documents that defined our country.

Despite all the distractions we thought we would get back to Camp Pickett. But as usual, the army brass had their own thoughts. We had no sooner returned to barracks than we were informed we would be going on maneuvers. This, the army decided, was away from creature comforts to some place very vile where we would play war games.

Our own particular hell was in several areas in Tennessee and Louisiana (we never called it anything except Lousy Anna). It was here we became intimately acquainted with lizards, snakes, spiders, alligators and various other varmints that all tried to take over whatever soft place we put our sleeping bags. It was sort of funny that we carried rifles with live ammunition with bayonets bared in Philadelphia, while in Lousy Anna we could not carry either one. We picked up sticks and used them to scare most of the wildlife away. There were some instances of snake and spider bites, but I did not hear of anyone being swallowed by a gator.

It was while we were having all this fun that the date June 6 arrived with the news that the Operation Overlord had started. Of course that was the news for the next several days. We did hear that our training would be picked up and probably our date to be included would be moved up.

It was when we got back to Camp Pickett that I remembered that my birthday was on June 7 and that my Dad's birthday was on June 9. It was the first time in my life I had been away from the family on my birthday. I phoned home and had a good talk with my Dad and Mother (never was allowed to call her Mom). Never did get a card from anyone at home which was sad. In fact, from June 1943 until Feb. 1945 I had a total of 4 letters from my folks and none from any friend or foe. I very seldom ever attended the mail call when the letters from home were passed out.

The training was tough. The weather was hot and muggy. As it was in Alabama, we spent hours going through infiltration courses, on the rifle and weapons ranges, climbing over obstacle courses and lunged at dummies with our bayonets.

Our passes gave us some time away from army stuff and we took advantage by visiting the small towns around the Camp as well as big ones like Richmond and Washington DC.

One day there was a notice on the bulletin board that there was to be a special dance in Richmond that had been arranged by a group of ladies who had daughters of about our ages. As we signed up we were told to make a special effort with our appearance, like haircut, shower, shave, shined shoes, etc. etc. About 40 signed up and were picked up in a bus and taken to a hotel where there was a huge ballroom. The ladies and their daughters were waiting for us.

The girls and their mothers were dressed in long evening gowns. The mothers sat at tables all around the room while the girls were in a bunch in the middle of the floor. It had been very carefully planned to let the young people dance, but there was no way a couple could slip out of eyesight of the mothers.

Some of the guys were less shy than others and they headed to the girls and started dancing. The band was playing all the current favorites and after each number the couples were urged to change partners so no one would be left out. My dance skills were pretty sad so I tried a couple of slow tunes. There was no way I could keep up with the currently popular jitter bug. This group of ladies had been coached to be pleasant and friendly but that was all. Towards the end of the evening I happened to be dancing with a tall girl that was quite pretty and as we did with all of them I asked her name. She said Virginia Lee. I did not believe her until I went with her to her mother's table and she verified that it was her real name and yes, she was a descendent of Robert E.

An interesting side light. After each musical number the girl would look you in the eye and say very sincerely "Thank Y'all. Ah enjoyed it". A small sample of Southern Hospitality. And it was nice to remember that although we were no longer gentlemen, we did remember that we had almost been and could still remember how to conduct ourselves. Every one of us who had been in Aviation Cadets made the rounds of the Mother's and thanked them for the evening and for sharing their daughters. Most of the Mother's had relatives or friends in the services and felt it was the least they could do to support those that were on the way to an unknown future.

Mixed in with the intense training, anxiety about the future, and getting ready to ship out, we were given overnight passes. A buddy with me in M company asked me if I would like to go to his home on Long Island. I thought that might be an interesting visit since I had not been to Long Island. I asked him how we would get there and back, and he said that would be no problem because his Dad would send a car down to pick us up. I wondered about the gas shortage. He said no problem. I wondered about the time frame since we would have to be back in 48 hours. He said no problem. After another hard day we cleaned up and went out by the gate. Lots of eyes bugged out, mine included. A 1940 Rolls Royce pulled up and a driver with a livery uniform jumped out and held the back door open for us. This was one of the models where there was a glass between the front and back seats. This chariot had leather on every surface including the side pocket that had cold drinks and some cookies for us to munch on. The Rolls was as quiet as their advertisement said. Henry said this was only for special occasions since he would be seeing his folks for the last time before going overseas.

His parents did their best to make me feel like a member of the family. I appreciated that effort because it had been a year since I had been home.

The ride back to camp in the vintage Rolls was the last bit of luxury I was to have for an unknown length of time.

There was one more trip we took that was interesting.

THREE DAYS IN NEW YORK—1944

It took a while to get adjusted to the new direction our lives were taking, but sometime late in the summer of 44 we spent our time at the rifle range.

Using the standard army combat rifle, the 30 caliber Garand, we fired a bushel basket of rounds at targets at 50, 100 and 500 yards. The three top winners of the contest on the final day would get a two day pass plus one. My friend from South Carolina came in first, I was second, and Bob Korte from Nebraska was third. None of us had ever been to New York City so that became the destination.

There were several ways to get from Camp Pickett, Virginia to New York. Even during the war busses and trains were often scheduled to take people on business that was important to the war effort. Service men and women could also ride if space was available. However, the easiest, cheapest, and fastest way was to hitchhike. In 44 hitchhiking was completely safe—everyone was eager to help a GI get from place to place. No GI would even think about taking advantage of anyone giving him a ride. I suppose there were rare instances of holdups, rapes, etc. but in the 3 plus years I was in the Army, I never heard of one.

So, we stood outside the gate, all dressed up for the first time in a long time in our Summer "suntans", complete with tie and shined shoes. We were picked up within minutes. The couples, probably in their 50's, were on their way to Washington to see their son who was a Captain in the Army, assigned to some military endeavor. Another thing you did not do during the war was ask specifically what a person did or where he was stationed. Nor did we say anything about our activities. The popular phrase at the time was "loose lips sink ships". Sounds corny now but was absolutely true then.

A short train ride from Washington to New York. We stood up all the way because of the crowded train. It was old equipment that had been resurrected. No air conditioning, the windows would not open and the seats were plain, wooden and hard. So it was not a hardship to stand.

We arrived at Grand Central Station. In those days it was everything the name implies. Even with wall to wall people it was like a palace. We found the USO booth and asked the lady about a place to stay for two nights. The only available place was at the YMCA. It was better than the barracks at Camp Pickett, and we could sleep, eat in their dining room, read local papers and use the swimming pool.

But we did not stay in the "Y" long. We had one full day and two evenings and wanted to see everything possible.

We had been told that afternoon was the best time to go to the top of the Empire State Building. They were right. The afternoon sun was lighting up one side of the skyscrapers while the other side was in shadow. Central Park, so much larger than I thought, it was like a huge green carpet. It was a perfect place to really get an idea of what New York geography was like.

As night fell we looked for a place to have dinner. The YMCA lady had advised us to ask in a big hotel. Not too far from the Empire State Building was the Waldorf Astoria. We had all heard about that famous hotel so we went in and inquired. Naturally, they said their dining was the best. We thought about the limited cash in our pockets but decided to give it a try. Surely there was something on the menu that would fit our resources.

When eating out we were under the same restrictions as anyone else because of the shortages. I do not remember the menu—56 years dulls the memory. I do have a strong memory of things being brought to the table that we did not order. Mostly things that we were not used to in the mess hall or doggy diners.

When the bill came (with a flourish) there was a note on the plate which we were almost afraid to read. But after getting the courage Bob opened the note and it read "Already paid in full including tip. Give Shickelgruber a kick in the pants for us". The waiter would not tell us who had paid nor would he take a tip. As we left we gave the whole room a wave of thanks.

We walked back to the "Y" and went to bed. Some people now would probably say what about the night life. There were many clubs and hot spots, but at that time none of us did any drinking and were pretty naive and green, so we passed that up.

Next morning we had a good breakfast and set out to see New York our way. Our intent was to walk Manhattan Island from top to bottom and from side to side.

We passed through many different neighborhoods. Everywhere we were treated with friendliness and good cheer. We walked through one area with many Jewish people. They kept cheering and clapping and trying to give us fruit from their sidewalk stands, bread from bakeries, etc. It took quite a while to get on our way.

Being from the Midwest and the South we did not really know what to expect as we walked through Harlem. But we need not have worried. This was before they started calling everyone brother and wearing strange clothes. They smiled, waved and seemed surprised and glad that we were there.

The walk took four hours end to end and two hours side to side, all at a good infantry pace.

The only place we had any problem was in Greenwich Village. It was getting towards late afternoon and we decided we were just a bit thirsty. When I said earlier that we did not drink that didn't mean coca cola or beer. The other two did drink a little beer, but I did not like beer (and don't to this day). Anyway we turned into a bar about midway in the block. There was a juke box playing some soft music (thank God there was no rock and roll to offend the senses). There was also some normal bar noises of conversation, etc. But it all stopped suddenly and there was dead quiet. When we started to pay some attention we could see that the bar was full of men with weird clothes and some dressed as women. The reek of perfume was over-powering.

The silence was broken and so was a bottle as one of the men took a beer bottle and holding it by the neck broke it against the bar. There were squeals of anger as almost the whole crowd rushed at us screaming obscenities. We quickly picked up three of the small cocktail tables and held them in front of us as a shield. It was a good move because we formed a barrier as we backed out. The noise was unbelievable. Then it got real scary when we heard some shouts from behind us. The cavalry had arrived. A group of Police and Shore Patrol filled in behind us and told us to back out slowly, put the tables down outside and get out of the area. They formed a line, raised their night sticks and went into the bar swinging the sticks, cracking heads right and left. The sergeant of Police told us to get lost "We'll take care of the damn queers". Times and attitudes have changed.

We were pretty quiet as we started back towards Times Square. We had a bite to eat at a small café then wandered along looking into store windows and talking about our recent experiences.

About 9 pm we were thinking about returning to the "Y". As we walked along we heard some good music down the block and decided to see what was going on.

I am glad we did because it turned out to be one of those things a person remembers all his life.

The music was coming out of a small place called Metropole. Remembering the Village experience we carefully entered into a different happening. The Metropole was not much more than a bar, but a far cry from the one earlier. It wasn't much more than 16 feet wide and about 40 feet long. The bar was all along the side extending the whole 40 feet. In back of the bar where the mirror and back-bar usually are was a platform not more than 4 feet wide. So with the bar and the platform the place for the public was no more than 10 feet wide. The place was not too crowded—yet. On the platform were men playing Dixieland, blues and big band stuff. Piano, Drums, Sax, Trumpet and Trombone. As we walked in two or three other GI's came in with us. They immediately switched into the Army Caisson song. Talk about a welcome.

Since I had been playing trombone in a dance band in Buffalo in my previous life, I went on down the bar and stood in front of the trombone player. A player, like which I had not heard before or since. They called him "Chief". He looked a little like he may have been of American Indian decent. Probably 6'4" and weighing a good 275. His tone was pure gold and he could play so soft and smooth you could have heard a pin drop, or he could lean on that horn and actually make the walls vibrate. We stood there and soaked up the music for at least 4 hours. Turns out they were all musicians from different bands, shows and night clubs. They all showed up on their own to just play for the fun of it.

I'll never forget those sounds of real musicians playing real music for real people. It was pure beauty!

It took a while for me to get to sleep reliving the events of the day, but we had to get back to reality and serious business of training to keep our promise to kick Schickelgroubers rear end. Leaving N.Y. the next day we went by the Stage Door Canteen. Movie Stars were regular visitors to help raise the moral of the soldiers. We were fortunate to visit with Joan Leslie. She was about our age and had a great sense of humor. She really lifted our spirits.

The hitchhike back to Pickett the next day was uneventful.

Sometime early in October we were told that it was time to move on. Our opportunity to get in the war was staring us in the face. Tension mounted as we were provided with new uniforms and duffle bags and told what to take with us and what we would have to leave behind. We could ash can the nixed stuff or send it home. I sent my trombone and some personal stuff back to Kansas.

Censorship became a fact. All letters we sent out had to be in an open envelope. Officers were assigned to read every letter to make sure there was nothing in them about our division, readiness for shipping out. Weekend passes were discontinued and all personnel were restricted to their company area.

The duffle bags were packed again and we were taken to Camp Kilmer, New Jersey. We went in old rickety busses, army trucks and some even took a short train ride. (Mostly Officers since they were more delicate). The busses were so old the springs had long since collapsed. The trucks were packed in the back so tight no one could have fallen out. Thankfully it was a short ride.

We did not have time to worry about what was happening. There were far too many lectures to attend. A Multitude of forms had to be filled out. Uniforms were inspected to make sure the proper insignia was sewed on. More inoculations and medical exams (and yes the infamous short arm). We were provided with gas masks and taught how to use them.

On October 13 the duffle bags were packed once more, and we staggered under the load as we boarded a train to be taken to the docks. It was raining when we arrived in Jersey City. From the train to ferry boats where we were again crammed into non existent spaces. The ride to New York harbor was done in complete silence.

Chapter 8

Convoy Across the Atlantic

The ferry boat snuggled against the dock and with full field packs, rifles on the shoulder, and full duffle bags we off loaded and lined up on the dock. It was dark and still raining. From someplace we heard an Army Band blaring patriotic march music. Red Cross volunteers went up and down the line serving doughnuts and coffee and wishing us good luck.

An officer appeared in front of us and started calling out names. When our last name was called we answered with "YO" and stepped forward and there was a gangplank and we finally were able to see the ship. The boarding process took several hours and as we got to our assigned bunks we tried to take a much needed nap. The excitement was too great so most of us listened to the noise of the harbor and wondered what would happen next. On deck the whole world was enveloped in a gray mist. We were sort of suspended waiting to feel the movement of the ship. When daylight came we were still tied up to the dock. The fog was too thick to move the ship. Soon it let up and the men were ordered below deck. We all crowded the portholes to look out.

On October 14, 1944 the 78th Division was on its way. By noon we had cleared the port and were out to sea. Gradually the horizon became filled with the other ships making our convoy. It was a grand and awe inspiring sight to see destroyers, supply ships, flat tops and a variety of ships all painted the dull blue/gray of war time. All of these other ships surrounded the three troop carriers with the 78th aboard.

Our three ships were the John Ericsson, formerly the Kungsholm which was the flagship, the Carnavan Castle, formerly a British merchant marine ship which had been refitted as a troop transport and another transport ship named the George O. Squier. I was aboard the George O. Squier.

Keeping watch on all this activity made the first day go very quickly. Getting used to the roll of the ship, finding our way to the galley, locating the almost adequate toilets. The next 8 days seemed to take forever. The scenery was the same each day with the only change being the roughness of the sea as the weather became less than pleasant.

I had never gambled but some of my buddies drug me into a game of 21. It was a way to spend the time. Not too bad an investment either. By the time we reached England I had won one hundred dollars which I immediately sent home to the folks as a coming up Christmas Present.

On the 8th day the convoy seemed to just sail away in all directions depending on what was on board and their ports of call.

Chapter 9

In Not So Jolly England

Two of our ships landed at Southampton and one landed at Plymouth. At both places the American troops were met by British officers and brass bands. The unloading process went pretty fast since we were pretty tired of the tight places on the ship. And there we stood for a couple of hours with those heavy duffle bags, rifles, gas masks, etc. Finally we were boarded on a train heading someplace. This train was small; the compartments were furnished with hard wooden upright seats. We squeezed in the best we could and wondered what's next. The train got underway and we crowded to the windows to see this country that had been bombed for the past 3 years. Everywhere we could see pill boxes, concertina wire and AA installations. AA is short for anti-aircraft guns. These were used to shoot German airplanes out of the air before they could drop bombs. So this is England!!!!!!! The train had been moving less than an hour when it stopped and we were ordered to disembark. We had been disembarked so many times we knew it meant "get off—now". Isn't it wonderful all the new words we had picked up this past year and some of them were not profane?

A sign in the station said BOURNEMOUTH. This didn't mean anything to the Americans but the British Officers seemed to think we should be happy to be there. After all, we found out, this was a very posh seaside resort area. We were taken to our assigned areas and after dumping our bags, rifles, etc. we had a chance to look around. We were put in hotel rooms that had been modified to house 4 soldiers in each room. There were cots and a small table and four small upright chairs. Let's hope that during peace time the furnishings were a little more comfortable. It was cold in the room and we wondered how they were heated. There was a small fireplace in each room that burned wood, coal, or anything else that burned. We had to go to the basement (I was on the 5th floor) to get the wood. It took the chill off the room, but we were never really warm. We spent a lot of the time going on night maneuvers or taking a 5 mile hike, or listening to lectures. This time the lectures were mostly about England and its history. And, of course, we learned about British money.

There were lots of things to do in the evening, such as pubs, dance halls, restaurants, theaters, tea rooms and of course girls.

I made it to London one time. London in the winter is foggy and cold. The fog was so thick that it was impossible to see your hand in front of your face. We were there during one of the fogs. We walked carefully down a street after getting off the bus. We were looking for a restaurant. All the stores had blackout curtains so no lights would show. Being careful to not run into someone we slowly went along following our noses. It became apparent that the doors were left slightly ajar so the smell of cooking would be an enticement to come to their restaurant. We went along for awhile until we came to one that we could not turn down. We went through the double curtains and found a wonderful little room that was typically English. The food was good and the people in the pub went out of their way to be friendly.

There was a newspaper on one of the tables and we looked through it to kill time. In this paper was an ad about a concert by Glen Miller. We wanted to go to this concert so we very carefully took to the sidewalk again looking for tickets. We found out soon that the tickets were sold out weeks ago. The auditorium was not far so we headed there in search of tickets. No luck and in addition we were told that there would be only one concert. Here we were with no tickets or hopes of getting any. The next best thing was to stand outside and listen to the music. The problem there was that there were hundreds more waiting in line—refusing to move.

I could tell the story, but in 1947 NBC put out a booklet about one of their most popular stars Johnny Victor. He was the voice of the radio show RCA VICTOR SHOW. He related stories of music and anecdotes—humorous, inspiring, and heart tugging.

I have a copy of that booklet and have copied this story of Glen Miller's last concert, although at that time Johnny did not know that this was Miller's last concert. The next day after the concert Miller boarded a small plane to fly to Paris which had just been liberated. He was to have arranged concerts there.

That airplane with Glenn Miller was lost over the Channel and has never been located.

We were in that line of a thousand music lovers that were able to get into the auditorium for that last concert. It was a doozy.

encore

One of the greatest tributes I ever heard was paid to the late Major Glenn Miller and his orchestra. Glenn and his boys were playing their first concert for Allied troops in bomb-riddled London. It was to be a single performance, and two thousand uniformed boys and girls filled the auditorium to capacity.

But outside, in the street, stood another two thousand troops, just as anxious to hear the band. Patiently they waited there, paying no attention to the MP's who told them there would be no second show.

The program was only half over when the red lights flashed inside the theatre, signalling an alert, and the familiar siren-scream wailed through the air. The Military Police and the theatre manager dashed to the street, to scatter the waiting crowd. Yelling and shouting they made their way along the line, begging them to take shelter—the buzz-bombs were on the way—it was no time to be stubborn!

But those uniformed ranks stood firm. Less than a block away a bomb landed, smashing buildings, scattering glass, and shaking the ground for blocks around. The Tommies and the GI's, the WRENS and the WACS stood their ground. Their hearts were jumping, but their feet never moved out of line.

When the dust settled the theatre manager mopped his forehead and went inside. Excitedly he told Glenn Miller what had happened. "Those crazy kids! I told them there wouldn't be any second show, and they just stood there with those bombs falling!"

Major Glenn Miller knew all about the hunger for music in hearts far from home—and he knew heroism when he saw it. That second show was a honey!

Late November in England was downright **COLD**. The practice maneuvers in the countryside were not pleasant. And this is where I drank my first full cup of coffee. There was only one way we figured that we could get warm enough so we would not turn into an ice statue. I had never really liked the taste of coffee and in the 30's there was not much demand for coffee, so a taste here and there was the most acquaintance I'd had with this brew. In an effort to get the warmth, we filled the canteen cups with steaming coffee from the big pots that were always going. We opened up our overcoats and put the hot cup between our sweaters and shirts, then buttoned the overcoats. It was probably only in our minds but it seemed to help. Little by little we would take a sip or two and then when it felt so good (and warm) going down, we started drinking full cups. There was no sugar or cream so it was strong and black.

We settled into a routine of training, and walking along the ocean and wondering what was coming next.

Chapter 10

Crossing The Channel to Le Havre

About American Thanksgiving time, everyone forgot that the English did not celebrate this holiday, so it slipped by. But about this time in late November we were taken back to Southampton and boarded ships for the crossing to the Continent. Those of us in heavy weapons and used jeeps for hauling ammunition were put on LST's with the jeeps lashed to the decks. An LST was a flat bottomed boat whose forward section did not have a point, but a flat hinged section that lowered to make a ramp to drive jeeps (or humans, or any kind of freight) on and off. We had two rows of these jeeps secured to the middle front part of the boat. The soldiers were to be berthed on a level below the main deck. There were bunks and a small kitchen where the meals were prepared. The trip was to take one full day with disembarking to take place at night. We were not told of our destination.

It was raining when we started the journey. Then as we went around the Southeast part of England the wind came up and the rain became worse. Just about due east of the White Cliffs of Dover the rain and wind came together and turned into a raging storm. They tried to feed us but no one was in the mood. The flat bottom of the boat pitched it around until all hands on the boat became sick. The ships captain, all the sailors and all of the soldiers. Word came that we were going to stay in one place facing the wind and try not to be blown off course.

No one wanted to go below deck. The pitch was much worse there and the smell of vomit made it even worse. I grabbed my gear and went to the main deck. I sat in our jeep and dressed in all the rain equipment I could find. Almost all of the soldiers followed along and there we sat—not for a day and a night, but for 3 full days. I moved from my seat maybe twice for two days to relieve myself and grab some crackers. The third day came with a light rain which was enough to clean up the deck as we made ready to land.

The other guys that went on larger ships had a hard time also, but not as bad as we had. They arrived a day earlier than we did and were happily settled on the plot of ground we had been assigned and which we called CAMP MUD.

We landed at Le Havre France. It was a mess. It was our first look at the total destruction caused by a battlefield. I was also a reminder of why we were here and realized that America had been spared. It was a quiet and somber group that made their way to Yvetot where Camp Mud was located. The French people were glad to see us and had a few laughs as we tried to pronounce the French names. Yvetot was a good example. The nearest we could come was "e toe"—not correct but camp mud was much easier.

Our Thanksgiving was celebrated (?) while standing in squishy mud, eating warmed over turkey out of our mess kits. Our overshoes were to be shipped on one of the convoy ships but did not arrive until our feet were cold and wet. We would change sox and put the wet ones around our bodies to dry out, but what good did that do when our boots were completely soaked?

Around Nov. 27 the jeeps were loaded with equipment and troops. There were two men to a jeep and they rode to our next destination in a long slow moving line. The rest of the troops were treated to a ride by train. The 40 and 8 cars had already become famous because they were used by the Germans to transport prisoners to concentration centers. I do not know who first called them 40 and 8 but it was natural since they were small and the joke was that they could hold 40 men and 8 horses. These box cars were dirty and smelled even worse. We were told at one of the lectures that the German's packed the cars so tight that there was hardly room to sit down. They left these people locked in the cars until they filled several cars—sometimes as long as several days. There was no food or drink and no toilet facilities. Many were dead when the train reached it's destination. These were the lucky ones. The survivors were used as slave labor and were worked until they too died.

We gathered in and around Tongres Belgium. It had been just a very short time since this area was liberated from the German's and the people regarded us as part of the liberating forces. The cheers and tears were somewhat embarrassing because we had not done anything yet. The troops rolled out their sleeping bags in barns and in half demolished houses. We were relatively warm again.

Now, the sounds of war were heard. Constantly the V-1 weapons roared through the sky. The buzz bombs sounded like a freight train in the distance.

Long streaks of sparks flew from their tails. We were told these were on their way to London. We were also told that although they had short wings they were not airplanes and could fail and could fall from the sky and explode. Sure enough once in a while we could hear one coming over and all of a sudden cut off. Then was the time to duck since they would come straight down. Several landed within 3 or 4 hundred yards with a tremendous explosion. We could hear anti aircraft batteries as they fired at the German bombers, also on their way to London.

Around the 7th of December we moved again. This time to Rotgen Germany where the 78th was attached to the First Army. The Division command post was set up and plans for the first attack were drawn up.

Again we moved, this time on Dec. 9th, to the outskirts of Lammersdorf Germany. Here we heard for the first time the names of Rollesbroich, Simmerath and Kesternich.

Chapter 11

Headlong Into Battle

Here is a quote from the book LIGHTNING THE HISTORY OF THE 78th INFANTRY DIVISION. Edited by The Division Historical Association. They had a quote that could say it better than I.

"On December 12 these men of the Lightening Division stood poised—ready. They were about to join in a living breathing sense of the long ranks of men who had built America with blood, and sweat, and pain. But the majority of the men lay in their shelters that night and wondered. The ground was covered with a thin crusted blanket of snow. The sky was overcast. Ahead of them lay a vast, formidable unknown. With them was a miserable coldness, a deep-rooted fear. They listened to the occasional bellow of heavy artillery pieces. Some men slept that night. Most of them lay awake."

It was at 0600 on the 13th when orders were passed down to move up to the line of departure. As we moved forward with as little noise as possible we could see dirty, tired soldiers moving back. These battle weary guys were the ones we relieved. Our ultimate goal was to capture the town of Schmidt and the Schwammenauel Dam. Both of these were critical to the success of Eisenhower's progress.

From this moment on it is hard to recall the exact sequence of action. The individual soldier is not consulted on where we will go or when. He is told when and where to dig in and all he can see of the battle is a narrow view of landscape where the enemy has set up his riflemen and machine guns and behind that the big long range artillery. Time slips by with only the cold and the sounds of battle as a constant. This narrative cannot tell where we were at any given moment because we did not know and now all these years later

I can only describe what I remember of the part I played. And exact times of happenings are blurred by time.

I can remember that morning of December 13 because of the noise. There is no way to describe the volume. Our artillery was shooting behind us, the enemy artillery was shooting at us, our mortars and machine guns were firing almost non stop, and the most terrible sound of all was the screams of those who were wounded. The sound was so great that we became disoriented until we stuffed anything we could get into our ears. Even then the sound could be felt all through the body. Through the whole day we fired more mortar shells than we did all the time we were in training. Our target was the line of pill boxes—the Siegfried Line. These pill boxes were built to take punishment. The walls were as much as twelve feet thick and the firing embrasures were so narrow firing into them from a distance was almost impossible. Our mortars had little effect, but we made them keep their heads down while our rifle companies were able to take them one by one.

Those 3 towns that I mentioned earlier (Bickerath, Simmerath and Kesternich) were next, along with Witzerath. It had taken 2 full days to move onto the plain where they were located. We had blasted them and they had blasted back. I think Simmerath was the first one we blasted with the mortars. Our jeep kept busy bringing ammunition to us and we kept the tubes hot. That was a good way to keep our hands warm. You would think we were in love with that mortar the way we hugged it.

In the few lulls while ammo was being reloaded, sights and sounds and smells started to be known. The smell of gunpowder filled the air. Then came that sound that we could never get used to—the screams of the wounded. It haunts me yet. Then the sight and smell of violent death, especially that first time which causes a soldier to be sick. He never gets used to it but puts up with it because it won't go away.

We learned very quickly to respect the Aid Men. They were the real heroes, constantly going out in the middle of a battle to help the wounded. They would administer the morphine shots and even amputate limbs, under heavy fire, often while they themselves were wounded.

As night time fell on the 15th we were told that in the next day or two we would be relieved and another Battalion would take over our positions. We welcomed the news and made sure our weapons were in place and operating since we wanted the incoming guys to be impressed.

At dawn on the 16th of December 1944 all hell broke loose. If we thought the 13th was noisy, it was like a pop gun against a cannon. Added to the noise was the trembling of the ground as von Rundstedt's tanks and armor started their blitzkrieg (or lightning war). The German's opened up with their biggest guns (one that was so big it had to be hauled on a specially made railroad flatcar). It made a horrible sound as it was fired and it was even worse as the huge projectile screamed on its way down. Just another quiet day at the office.

Our Regiment was pulled back and then sent around the North edge of the bulge. It was a twenty mile march only this time it was for real. My spotter had been hit by a stray rifle shot in his upper are. It was what was referred to as a flesh wound. (Anything short of knocking the whole arm or leg off was considered a flesh wound). His wound had taken a fair portion of his shoulder muscle. They doped him up and put a bandage on him and he became a walking wounded. As we had to take our weapons with us it was necessary to make sure the 40 pound base plate moved with us. I said I would take it for awhile, but when I passed it on, the others could not take all the weight. So there I was, 40 pounds of base plate, 40 pounds of tube, 50 pounds of backpack, a belt with 10 pounds of ammunition and eight or ten hand grenades. In all probability more than a hundred and fifty pounds.

What the leaders did not know was that my feet had started to go bad with what became trench foot and it was painful to walk. I wanted to drop out, I prayed that I would just stumble and roll over in a ditch and stay there for the duration. But no such luck. It's surprising what you can do when someone (many someone's) is shooting at you with intent to do damage. Thankfully a unit of a British force relieved us as soon as we established our position of the flank of the bulge. It took a day just to draw a breath that didn't hurt someplace. Thankfully, the feet were just starting their decline and when we went back on the line I could navigate OK.

At this time we held back waiting for some other units to get into place before going into the middle of the bulge with the goal of cutting it in two pieces and disrupt their supply lines.

By this time the C rations were getting a little monotonous and we were beyond hungry. The next morning a poor milk cow wandered into our area. It was her big mistake. One of the guys took a 45 cal. Pistol and put 6 shots directly into her head at a one foot range. It took all 6 before she would drop. But she did make about 50 guys some nice steaks.

The German's soon found out where we were and tried their best to keep us from cutting into their plans. The weather was cold—usually between 0 and 20 degrees. Some snow and sleet was falling and we had to dig our mortar emplacements and our individual fox holes. It was easiest to dig our fox holes long and narrow and no more than 2 feet deep. It kept us below ground level to avoid shrapnel and small arms fire. Nothing would help if there was a direct hit from the artillery. The mortar emplacements were more elaborate. The holes we dug were about 5 feet across and 4 or 5 feet deep. The ground was frozen so it was difficult digging with our little fold-up trenching shovels. We then found limbs that had been blown off trees and put them over the back half of the hole. That was cover for us from the snow, rain, etc. It really did not help, but we thought it did. The mortars would then extend just past the limbs and we could raise and lower the tube for distance control. They could reach a maximum of about 2500 yards and could traverse side to side about 30 degrees. I remember one afternoon when we were pouring shells into one of the villages where we were softening up the German's for our riflemen. The ground beneath the base plate was soft and every time we fired a shell the recoil pushed the base plate further into the soft soil. That made the tube rise up just a touch at each firing. After about 50 shells, I moved over so we could trade places to keep from getting cramped in one place. I noticed that as the shells exited the tube they were very, very close to the limbs on the top of the hole. If one of the fins of the shell caught on one of the limbs and misdirected the path of the shell it would be curtains for any number of people. We quickly put things right and continued our shelling. Our ammunition man said we had put about 300 shells out that afternoon. The tube was red hot and had taken about all the heat it could without becoming distorted and unusable. We got a new tube the next morning.

The next night was when the German's decided to wipe us out for good. The fields were like patchwork. Trees surrounded each 5 or 10 acre farm. The 88's started just after dark when we were trying to get something to eat and try to get comfortable in our fox holes. The bombardment went on for an hour or so and seemed to be close, but we were not being hit. The next morning we could see that they thought we were in that next field and had gone up and down the field like a plow and had covered every foot of land with their bombardment. If they had known we were in the next field we would have been wiped out. The 88's were deadly (and thus scary).

The next night they sent in the paratroopers. It had started out as a typical cloudy and rainy night. You could not see 2 feet in front of your face. Luckily for me just as we could hear the airplanes coming, the clouds passed over and a weak moon could be seen. Suddenly we saw all those shapes drifting down. It took about a millisecond to figure out we were in trouble. We always lay on our backs in the foxholes with rifles at our side. Those of us in heavy weapons carried the 30 cal. Carbine and a 45 cal. pistol side arm.

The light was just good enough that we could see to start picking them off as they came down. They had thought to take us by surprise, but they were really sitting ducks. The few that survived were taken prisoner, relieved of their weapons including grenades, and forced to lie down until we could get them back to the MP's. The ones that did not survive were also relieved of all their belongings except identification so the proper notification was made for headquarters. There were two officers that did not make it. I took a small case from one of them that contained a set of small matched pistols—very fancy. I don't know why he would have had them unless he thought they would be stolen by his buddies if he left them behind. The thing that most of us took was the silk parachutes. We cut them into long strips and wound them around our middles to help us keep warm. I brought a piece of it home with me and ended up using it as a background for my medals display. Later we found out that this was just a small group of elite paratroopers sent in to disrupt our counter offensive. We accounted for all of them. I never did get the complete count, but it was in the neighborhood of 10 killed and 20 captured. We did not lose anyone.

The set of pistols I carried until I was sent back to the aid station. I asked a friend of mine to send them to my home. All I ever got was an old German bayonet that I had never seen before. So much for friends.

As we went forward, we were getting near Christmas. The weather had been bad since we started and our aircraft had not been able to get out to give us any close support. The Air Force had also been unable to make any great raids on Berlin and the Industrial part of Germany.

We received another break. Christmas day dawned clear but still cold. The skies were filled from horizon to horizon with all that air power. Big planes on the way to Berlin, P-38's swinging underneath for protection, and our fighter support had arrived. They finally could see the extent of the German offensive and could direct how best to counter it.

All of a sudden there was a period of quiet. We were busy digging in to protect the ground we had wrestled away from the German's. The German's were busy building the defenses they had had in place for many months. There was one area that was two hills about a mile apart with a valley in between. We were on one hill; the German's were on the other. We could see each other moving along the tops of the hills.

I was acting as forward observer, sitting on the hill, leaning against a tree watching for any sign of change in the pattern that might signal the start of some action by the enemy. There was a road of sorts close to the bottom of the opposite hill where once in awhile a vehicle would go along. On this occasion there was a German supply truck tooling along as if he did not have a care in the world. I called back to ask permission to fire a couple rounds of mortar at him-just for harassment. Since there were occasionally burst of fire at each other, and they knew where we were anyway, I was told to go ahead. I called back to my gunner and gave him the coordinates I thought would get close to the truck. The first round was the right distance, but hit a hundred yards behind him. I made some adjustments and the second round hit him square. The truck just literally came apart at all seams. There were many small objects, all about the same size, flying through the air. We could not identify them right away. No German's went out to investigate. That night there was a flurry of activity from the enemy side and we sent a couple of tanks in to take care of the two machine gun nests we knew were there. This pushed them off their hill and we moved on and took over their position. On the way we stopped by the truck. It had been loaded with cans of peas. They were everywhere. The driver of the truck was not found, so they probably came to get him under cover of darkness.

We like to think that part of the quiet was because it was Christmas Eve. The night before we could hear the German's singing Christmas Carols.

Our Battalion was pulled back (we rotated) to Roentgen which was in Germany. Two or three things had been planned for us—Christmas dinner with all the trimmings, and a new set of clothes, showers, health check and rest.

The first was the clean up of a bunch of very dirty and smelly guys.

It's worth a re-telling.

The Special Services people had set up a huge tent, big enough for a couple hundred people. Along both sides they had rigged shower heads that were fed by huge tanks that were heated by gas fired heaters. We came into the tent, took everything out of our pockets, took all of our clothes off and threw them in a big container. You ask "what about the parachute pieces and any personal stuff?" We all had our original barracks bags that were stashed in the rear areas. We had our serial numbers stenciled on them so we could distinguish our own. We were warned ahead of the showers to put anything personal in our bags and leave them in the truck.

We were let into the tents about 100 at a time. 50 naked, dirty guys on one side and 50 naked, dirty guys on the other. We were handed a bar of soap when we went into the showers. And we stayed there until they had to make us leave. Few things have felt as good as that shower, washing off sweat, dirt, blood, and just plain grime that had been ground in since before December 13th.

As we left the showers at the other end of the tank we were handed a towel, comb and a set of OD's. We also received two set of long underwear and 3 pairs of socks and a pair of shoes and overshoes. When we had started, we had long overcoats, but when it became apparent that we could get mistaken for German's who had longer long coats, we were issued field jackets.

In the next tent were some doctors and nurses who gave us the once over and checked our mouths and teeth for dysentery, and took care of all the minor cuts and abrasions. Then we put on our clothes and left this tent. There was another tent where we were given a butch haircut (which most of us had already, but needed to have it done again).

One of the wise guys asked a nurse if she had any problem being around all those naked guys. Her comment was "This is a virgin's prayer".

We woke up early Christmas morning earlier than usual because of a rumble like a thousand motors. We rolled out of our sleeping bags and looked up to see the most beautiful wonderful sight and sound. The weather up to this point had been overcast and our Air Force could not see many of their targets. But this Christmas day dawned clear with a welcome sun rising ahead of us. The whole sky as far as you could see was filled with our planes heading towards Berlin. The B17's were flying in close formation and P38's were flying protection and swinging under the 17's as if on a pendulum.

All of a sudden we were not tired, cold and hungry anymore. We shouted and lots of us cried as we waved them on, urging them to blast Berlin into rubble.

Now we were ready for the next phase of our Christmas: the promised dinner. We had been eating C and K rations for so long it was going to be a treat to eat like a human again. The dinner was as promised—all the trimmings. The only problem was that almost all of the food was canned or hydrated with water so it could travel and not spoil. It was all much better than what we had been eating. But trouble came. The sweet potatoes probably were spoiled since almost every one of us became sick. The trips to the latrine were constant. I got so bad, and the slit trenches smelled so bad, a bunch of us took our trenching tools and headed for the open field next to where we had spread our sleeping bags in barns and sheds. One of my several close calls was in that field. I was doing my thing in the hole I had dug when a German Stukka fighter came over and strafed right down the middle of the field. The two rows of machine gun bullets went on each side of me and several others, we were too sick to care. He only made one pass—probably laughing so hard he could not keep his attention on his flying. We laughed later!

The next day we kept getting shot at by a sniper. For a while we could not locate him, but pretty soon he became greedy and we were able to spot him in a church steeple about a block away. A lieutenant came up to us and said that since we were able to take out that truck we should be able to knock that guy out of the steeple. It took two rounds, but we knocked the top off the steeple and put him out of commission. Only it was not just one sniper. One was a he and the other was a she. They were both alive and after getting some first aid were sent back to spend the rest of the war resting in a POW area.

The other interesting thing about our stay here was the prototype of the VW. It had the name on it and was covered up in the back area of the small factory that was nearby. VW of course stands for the Volkswagen (car). It did not look much like the bug we know, but was along the same lines. My camera had been busted by a shell somewhere along the way, so I could not bring back a picture.

That was Christmas 1944. A Chaplin made a few remarks, we sang some carols, and we decorated a small spruce tree with food cans, packages and some of the other stuff things came in. We thought about those at home and wondered what they were doing.

That night it was time to pack up, make sure all our weapons were ready, take one more glance at the tent where we took our showers and get ready to start out again. Still wondering about all those virgins. The rest of December was a struggle. The German's had concentrated almost all of their assets into the bulge and we were outnumbered and out tanked. We had one thing going for us. They were getting short of fuel and were depending on reaching Liege, Belgium where most of the allied fuel reserves were stored. If they had made it, the war would have lasted for at least another year. We were committed to their failure.

We had just set up our positions so we would not be surprised by the German's. Our mortar was in a deep hole with branches over the top for camouflage and we were doing all those things that could not be done while in a battle. Things like taking a deep breath, washing sox and underwear, taking a much needed nap and catching up on where we had been and where we were going. It was wasteland where we had been and no way of knowing where we were going. There were lots of guesses anyway.

Jeeps were used for a lot of things. All of those things were important, like carrying ammunition and serving as wheels for what we called runners. These guys spent most of their time taking messages from Ike to all the division commanders. One of these runners was hit by an 88 a short distance from where we were resting. He was hurt enough that he had to be sent back to an aid station. The runner needed major surgery. I was sitting in the seat of our jeep because it was a lot softer and warmer than the ground. Two Officers came up to where I was sitting and asked if I would like to do a small errand for them. The Officer, a Major, said he had a message that should get to a small village a little bit south of where we were. I was surprised when he asked me instead of telling me I would drive him in our jeep. Our Officer said it would be OK and that was good enough for me. Anything to have a change of activity.

I never learned the Major's name but as always the word SIR was enough. We jumped in the jeep and headed out. We bounced, slid and chugged along the road that was not more than two ruts filled with snow and ice and pockmarked with the craters made by direct artillery hits, both theirs and ours.

After we had been going for awhile he told me we were going to Bastogne. Had I known that this little village was to have its own place in history; it would have made me more observant of those we later met there. A lot of words and names come to me now—General McAuliffe, courage, faith and a will to persevere, and the now famous one word reply to the German's who wanted the 82nd Airborne to surrender **"NUTS"**

We plowed on and it was beginning to get dark. We cut our lights and followed the shadow line between snow and trees-sometimes on the road and sometimes off. I later estimated the distance to be roughly 20 miles. The clouds broke up a little and there was a faint moon that gave us at least a bit of visibility so we were able to increase our speed a bit. The road was in bad shape and it wound around the hills in tight turns. On one of these turns we were near the top of a hill and there in front of us was a German soldier and we heard the chilling and unforgettable sound of a burp gun. This small machine pistol could fire a tremendous amount of rounds in a second. I hit the clutch, second gear and foot feed all at the same time. The flat sliding spin and acceleration kicked rocks at the Kraut getting ready to fire another burst. By the time he figured out what had happened the jeep was under a full head of steam going in the opposite direction. I said a little prayer of thanks to the inventor or the burp gun. Something caused him to invent a device that spit out that amount of rounds and at the same time be totally inaccurate.

The noise woke up a crew on an 88 and a couple of shells were dropped on the road behind us. It was obvious that they did not know our exact location since they could put an 88 shell in your hip pocket from a half mile if given half a chance.

The Major did not say a word for a minute and I sneaked a look at him. He looked like someone dumped a sack of flour on him. I was as scared as he was. Another minute passed and finally, looking straight ahead, and in a quiet voice he said, "Still haven't seen one of those contraptions do any damage". Now there was a man cool under fire.

We pulled into another side road that according to the map swung around and came into Bastogne from another angle. We did not want to try to get into town in the middle of the night for obvious reasons, so we pulled over under some trees and took a short nap. It snowed on us a little before daylight as we continued on. Right at daybreak (at least by our watches) we saw Bastogne from the top of a hill nearby. There was no doubt about this being a USA held town because the German's were laying down a barrage of artillery that wouldn't let anyone stick his head up. The blasts were setting fires all over the village and the red flashes were sending colorful rainbows against the cloudy sky. It was as deadly as beautiful. We watched and felt sorry for those poor guys in the village. There was probably no place for them to hide.

Just as quickly as it started, the barrage went quiet. The Major said "let's go and don't stop for anything". It took about 3 minutes to get inside the crumbling walls and not one single shell dropped in the meantime.

They guys on guard duty signaled us through as if we were expected. As we entered we could see that recovery was being made after the shelling. People were being accounted for, damage was being checked. The Major asked a soldier coming out of a damaged house where we could find the General. He motioned over his shoulder to the corner of a building close by. This corner of a solid but damaged building was pretty much intact. The Major jumped out of the jeep, told me to hide the jeep and he headed into the building. I found a mound of rubble that was high enough that the jeep would fit behind. I waited.

About 4 or 5 minutes later the Major came out with a soldier with stars on his shoulders. The General had the envelope the Major had been carrying. We were just about ready to go back to our starting point when there was a distant WHUMP and the whistle of incoming artillery. The round landed less than a block away and the force of the blast pushed us back into the building. It was obvious why this was headquarters. The basement walls were at least 2 feet thick and were probably the safest place in Bastogne.

I have mentioned it earlier, but being here on the receiving end I developed more respect of the Artillery. While I was in this basement with a General, a Major and several other Officers, I had a sudden thought about the sound and fury.

Just imagine a giant wearing corduroy pants walking on top of a huge bass drum Swish . . . boom . . . swish . . . boom . . . Then he moves over a little bit and walks back parallel to the first route. Back and forth until the whole area has been covered. And that is only the firing. On the receiving end it is a continuous boom that shakes the earth.

We were unable to talk above the unbelievable noise. The dust and plaster and pieces of masonry came down over everyone. Even the stone building shook as the shells came marching past. Everyone knew that a direct hit would send tons of ancient building stone crushing through into the basement. Every one was now coughing because of the dust.

I offered up a prayer and I know many of the other did also. I know this is not where the phrase, "there are no atheists in fox holes" originated, but it certainly could have.

The shelling continued for twenty minutes (or so) then quit as abruptly as it had started.

The General jumped up first and ran up the stairs and pushed the door open, which was now hanging from one hinge. The square was a mess. He ran quickly across to what was left of the smaller building, pushing the door aside and he called down the small flight of stone steps. Plenty of old plaster and thousand year old dust had settled around them, but it appeared that none had been hurt.

He requested a report as soon as possible on the fate of all his troops. Soon the reports were coming in and most were favorable. Those old buildings with walls twelve to twenty four inches thick could take a lot of punishment. There were some casualties which brought a tightening of the lip of the General. A quiet command and a squad of special services people headed out to take care of the wounded and the dead.

The Major and I threw some debris out of the jeep and it was time to get out of Dodge.

The trip back was in daylight so we could speed up the return. The speed is what saved us. We were barreling along and as we went around a tight curve there in front of us were 4 or 5 German's, probably on patrol, but this time they had rifles. They were as surprised as we were and did not react soon enough. I stomped on the gas and we plowed right through them. They had made the fatal mistake of standing in the middle of the road instead of near a ditch they might have been able to jump into. They went flying in all directions. I know the jeep hit two of them and there were a couple of shots fired. It was not until we got back that we found the two bullet holes on and near the left hand headlight. We kept moving as fast as possible and made it safely back with no more surprises.

On our return Special Services located a jeep so the Major could get back where he belonged and I could get back to where I belonged, pounding another small village into rubble with mortar shells.

The month of January was one of the coldest on record in Europe. We lived it day after day with hardly any relief. We had on our same clothes, in fact never took them all the way off or we would have frozen. By day, as we were advancing or moving from place to place to dig another mortar emplacement, we would sweat from the exertion. Then, at night as we tried to hunker down in shallow fox holes, the sweat would turn to ice. You could hear us crackle as we walked. Once in a while, a clean dry shirt would arrive with the food—another time a clean pair of pants or long johns. I do not remember being completely warm during that time.

But several things happened during January that either relieved the situation a little bit, or made it worse. Rather than day to day details I think a couple of remembered incidents would be interesting. Interesting to me trying to remember, but hopefully not boring to you trying to read through all this.

As I said before—"so be it".

Sometime during that month, General Eisenhower, General Hodges of the 1st Army and General Bradley of the 8th Army were on an inspection tour of the front. They were driven by the now famous lady who was speculated to be on more than friendly terms with Ike. Actually, she was quite nice to talk to and was passably pretty. General Parker, the 78th's commander was showing them around and they were passing by our mortar hole in the ground. About that time, the German's came through with one of their famous barrages and everyone hit the ground. The Generals included. Eisenhower and Hodges were the closest to us and jumped right into our hole. There was not much room, but we learned how to make ourselves as small as possible. My gunner that day was in the hole with me and we had just been setting up our firing schedule. So that made four of us in a hole big enough for maybe 3 1/2. After the initial shock of having Generals with us, I thought we would be ignored. But both of them asked questions about us, where we came from, our target that we had been setting up, and how we were fairing. I got as far as telling them I was from Kansas. So was Eisenhower and he got downright friendly, asking about my hometown and places we knew. I remembered to throw in a "sir" now and again. After the barrage was over and everyone and everything had been inspected to determine the damage, Ike came back with a photographer from Stars and Stripes. I heard later that there was an article in S & S that read "Kansas soldiers meet in foxhole". I have never seen it.

The battles raged back and forth. The German's had the advantage because they had from 1918 to prepare defenses for their homeland. It was our job to route them out. There were deep bunkers everywhere. They were sometimes deep enough to hold several soldiers and had been fixed up for a fairly comfortable living situation. Some even had small stoves and boxes to hold supplies, and of course, the machine guns and mortars. We developed a routine to clear out these obstacles. They had all the approaches covered so it was not easy. We would hunker down behind some protection and holler out "what is the name of the New York baseball team?" If there was silence or the answer was not right we would bring up a bazooka or a flame thrower. Then a couple of hand grenades would be tossed in just to make sure. It became hairy at times because some of our guys had already been there and were enjoying the comfort (and warmth) of the bunker. It was an endless task, WAR, after all, was fought foot by foot, house by house and bunker by bunker. There were no short cuts.

We also had to watch out for German's wearing American uniforms. Lots of tense moments before we let soldiers pass, certain the uniforms contained Americans. If a wrong answer was given to a simple question they were marched to the rear to the prisoner holding areas.

Once we had penetrated the Siegfried Line and the villages that were part of it, we had to maintain our positions. More than once we had to fall back and go around, and come in behind the attacking forces. This is what made it so confusing. All the small villages looked the same and they had to be taken and retaken several times. We were back in Kesternick going from house to house. We also rescued several of our guys who were hiding out with severe cases of trench foot and wounds. They had been left behind when the last group went through and they were not mobile enough to move.

We were in the middle of a terrific exchange of fire. The big guns on both sides were working overtime. We were putting about 10 rounds a minute into the mortar and machine gun emplacements of the enemy. They were putting at least that many into our position, as well as those blasted 88's. The medics were busy with their stretchers (hopefully on both sides). The Krauts were out to take over the world, and we were equally determined to keep them from it.

As far as I could determine, we had cleared a couple of the big hurdles and were aiming at the next one which was the Roer River. Holding back the river were two dams, the Schwammenauel and another smaller one up river.

It was very important that we capture the dams before the German's had a chance to blow them up.

But first, we had to get through this tough battle we were in.

It had started at daybreak and was still continuing. The noise was awesome, the cold was so bad that the weapons were freezing up, and the cold rain and wet snow were coming down.

I happened to be sitting on the edge of our mortar emplacement, looking for the ammunition man to arrive. We were almost out of shells.

We could tell from the whistle of the incoming shell that it would be close and we all hit the ground. I was facing the mortar next to ours and saw the shell make a direct hit. The resulting spurt of dirt and debris was red and we knew someone had been hit. Two of us crawled over to the hole. There was only one person in the hole. He was wounded badly, but we did not know the extent of his wounds until we extracted him from the pieces of mortar, limbs, dirt and worst of all pieces of human. It was not the first time we had seen this, but this time the pieces belonged to a close friend. We knew nothing could be done about him so we kept digging the other one out.

It was obvious that he would not make it either. His intestines were spilling out and one arm hung by just a sliver of flesh. He was conscious and from the look on his face he knew that it was bad. I gave him a shot of morphine and cradled his head on my lap while he tried to keep his intestines from falling to the ground. It was too late for that—they were already dirty. The ground under him was turning red. The morphine took most of the pain away for the moment. He and I talked about home and our families, and he asked me to tell them he did not cry. He died there before the medics arrived. I cried for him.

When the medics came they brought the body bags—we called them sleeping bags—just one less reminder of how fragile life really is. The medics put him more or less back together, secured his personal belongings and put them in a bag with his dog tags. Then they put him in the body bag and zipped up the bag. The sound was so final that I had to remember to take a breath. At least he was out of sight as they carried him to the truck that was already half full of full bags. They threw him on the pile like a log. Another mother would die inside as a telegram was delivered to another door in another town back home.

There was not enough of the other guy to cart away. We searched the area until we found his dog tags and his dented helmet which had been discolored by the explosive powder. The medics carefully put these in a bag so they could account for another casualty. We had a great respect for the medics. It was a terrible job, but for the most part they did this job with dignity and compassion.

This was not the only instance of close friends being lost, but this story is enough to give the reader an idea of what it was like, day after noisy, bloody day.

A half hour later the noise started again, and we went back to trying to give the German's more grief than they gave us. Those terrible messengers of death were again going back and forth.

It's now a couple of days later here in 2002, and I am just getting back to the computer. I almost deleted the last page a couple of times. I also thought that I should just end this story. But I am better now, and writing about what have been nightmares from time to time, seems to have eased some of my thoughts. My experience was not unusual. There were actually thousands of similar moments experienced by thousands of guys that were young and in the same boat. If it was not actually hell, it is a quick glimpse into it.

To continue the story—an hour later we were again pumping shells at the enemy. That battle ended as they all did—abruptly. It was surprising that we did not have more casualties.

The cold continued and so did the decline of my feet. I was now wearing two pairs of socks and overshoes. I had thrown away the shoes that would not fit my swollen feet.

One of the stories of the cold made the rounds. A platoon leader was making a last check before an attack when he saw a private trying to get his attention. "What's the matter?" whispered the Lieutenant. "Sir, my fingers are so cold I can't move'em." The Lieutenant asked "do you want me to send you to the rear?" The guy answered "no just unlock my piece".

The battle of the dams started. The big dam held back an estimated 22 billion gallons of water. The problem was that the allies were trying to cross the Roer all along its route, and if the German's blew the dam, it would release all that water in a flood that would wipe out thousands of our troops all up and down the river as they tried to cross.

So the attack by the 78th Division, and more specifically our 309th Battalion, was launched on Feb. 5 at 0300. We were to capture a barracks and staging area that held many of the elite troops the German's were still relying on to continue their assault.

It was still cold and it was black dark at 0300. The riflemen were leading as we moved through the heavily wooded area. We fell over bushes, walked into trees, unable to see what was ahead. We were slowed down by the obstacles. As the light started dispelling the dark we could move with more certainty. As the dawn broke the riflemen moved in on the huts of the barracks area, while we set up our mortars and zeroed in on the front edge.

We took them completely by surprise. Some were still asleep and others were having breakfast. It was easier than we had anticipated. We sent long lines of prisoners back to our lines.

But no rest for the tired, hungry and still cold troops. It was to our advantage to press the attack before the enemy could reorganize. The plan was to try to cross the Roer down stream, head north to try to take the East side of the dam. This plan was cancelled when it was discovered that the river rapids were too swift for a crossing, and the German's had an extensive defensive line overlooking the river. The change called for our Battalion to continue the attack and for the 9th Division to come in from the North.

This was difficult terrain to be fighting in. A large quantity of material was of necessity concentrated in a small area. The roads were not too good to start with, but now the hilly, muddy roads were a mess. Tanks dug deeper and deeper in the mud. Messenger jeeps and other vehicles, some carrying chow, were having trouble getting through. But the offensive was taking shape.

On the 6th of Feb. the 310th moved out and our battalion followed for backup and to alternate.

The battle was a bitter one. The German's had every inch zeroed in with mortars and artillery. The riflemen charged on—we followed, laying down a heavy concentration that kept progressing ahead of the riflemen. It kept the German's off balance and unable to reorganize.

The details of the battle have been told many times and the book I have called "Lightning" tells how the battle strategy was developed.

The riflemen slid down the face of the dam and surprised the ones on guard there. The engineers followed and checked out the dam, although still under fire. Only an outlet valve had been blown and the dam was captured and with the fall of the town of Schmidt, the bulge was broken and we were on the way to the Remagen Bridge across the Rhine and on to Berlin.

From Dec. 13th to Feb. 10th the 78th had cleared over 35 square miles of Siegfried defenses, captured 16 towns and 2700 prisoners. The 78th used 242 million rounds of .30 caliber ammunition, 10,000 rounds of 81 mm mortar shells. Ordinance furnished 159,000 pounds of TNT; engineers had placed 28,400 antitank mines, 3500 antipersonnel mines. The Quartermaster's issued 415,000 gallons of gas and over a million rations. The Signal Company had lain over 2,000 miles of telephone wire. The most important statistic I cannot verify, but I heard when it was over 500 dead and 6000 wounded were removed from the fighting.

Most of the next week or two was spent in securing our position and the dams that had been captured. We had yet to make a full scale crossing of the river because of the heavy resistance on the high ground by the elite troops that had been cut off and pushed back to another line of defense they had prepared long ago. They were a seasoned army and were tough to get out of any place they were entrenched. Besides, I think they were sore because we took the dam before they could blow it up.

Reminds me of a side story. The British were on our North and at one time, briefly, we had been attached to the British force. We were back with our own 78th and had secured the dam and were keeping the German's at bay with our artillery and mortars. The British were sent in to guard the dam to relieve our troops so we could keep the pressure up.

If you have ever read any stories about the British military, you will recall that they do things differently.

One of their routines is to have tea mid afternoon, no matter what else is going on. They built a fire in the middle of the dam and were brewing their afternoon tea. Instead of spreading out to minimize wiping out a whole bunch of troops at one time, they were all gathered together in a big loud social setting. We wondered why the German's didn't blast them from their positions on top of the hill on the other side. Then, at night, instead of being quiet and whispering to keep the enemy from knowing exactly were they were, they marched up and down the dam with their steel hob-nails in their boots.

Toward morning, the German's did lob a few mortars on the dam, but I think it was because all the noise was keeping them awake. I know that we cheered the German's when the British had to break up their funny ways.

During this time we sent out many patrols all along the river probing for weak spots in their defenses. We also sent out many diversion strikes to see how they reacted. It was a time to gather our strength, material, fuel, etc. for the next big push. This time it would be to cross this natural barrier in our path.

In moving from place to place, up and down the river we discovered two underground factories manned by slave labor. The factories were there to build aircraft and other military goods. The men in these factories were of course not paid any wages. They were paid with plenty of punishment and were provided with little or no food, and the living conditions were not by any stretch of the imagination what you could call living. Most people will take better care of their dogs. Their beds were just a piece of cloth they rolled up in and they slept on the dirt floors. The plan was to take these people, that were not soldiers, from their homes and put them in these places to be worked until they could no longer stand. The beatings and malnourishment caused them to last just a short time. They were then shot, if not already dead, and buried in shallow graves. The men were all skin and bones with bruises and cuts and what looked like whip marks all over. They had very little clothes and must have suffered from the cold.

They were glad to see us, but so far gone and so beaten down they hardly looked up.

We wondered how a human could treat another human in this manner. Later on, we found out they could do far worse when the allies liberated the concentration camps in Poland and other places under German control.

We hoped that the husband of the Timmerman girl in Tongres had not suffered the same fate. The chance though was great that he had. Our other hope was that we could end this with a victory, so that 90% of the world would not be like those slaves.

I was not to see the crossing of the Roer.

It was on a hill overlooking another little valley that my tour of duty came to an end. I was on forward observer duty with a Corporal from the artillery doing the same thing. We were sitting under a line of trees—the last line until the top of the next hill where the German's were. I was changing my socks again and wondering how much longer I would be able to walk without limping. We would send a shell over to their line and they would send one of theirs back to ours. We were only keeping each other awake.

One of theirs hit high up in one of the nearby trees, we called it a tree burst, and along with some branches a piece of shrapnel came whistling down and stuck straight into my upper leg. It wasn't big and it didn't hurt much, but it did bleed a bit. I could not pull it out. A medic was just behind us and he came up and gave me a morphine shot and sent me back to the aid station. It was not too far back since we had been more or less in the same area for a while and the Quartermaster's with the food, the ammunition carriers, and the aid stations were able to keep up.

On the way back, as I was walking along side a burned out tank, one of those darned 88's hit just at the front side of the tank. The right hand corner of the tank saved me from real damage. The concussion flipped me over and up against a telephone pole that had been damaged earlier. Somehow I got some splinters in my back and was knocked out.

I woke up on a cot where I had been placed by the medics who had picked me up. A nurse was cutting off my clothes. That must have been a tough job since they had at least two weeks worth of dirt, sweat, ice, blood and no telling what else on them. She threw them in a big can with what looked like more of the same. They were no doubt burned as soon as they could fill the can. A male intern was taking off my galoshes at the same time. The nurse painted around the piece of steel sticking out of my leg with a disinfectant and proceeded to sponge me off. I had been pretty careful to keep my body as clean as possible even though I had to work out of a helmet in cold water and a pinch of soap that came with our rations. So her work was not as hard as you would think.

Chapter 12

The Voyage Home

Shortly after I had been put in a bunk with a backless gown to cover me, a military doctor came by inspecting the most recent newcomers. He looked at the piece of steel and then at my feet and said "We can fix the leg wound in a jiffy if it is not too deep, but your feet are a mess. You won't be doing any more fighting". This was (I think) Feb. 17th, 1945.

I took in this news with mixed emotions. On one hand I was glad to know that I would be out of the cold and away from that awful noise and smell. On the other hand I had the terrible feeling that I had let my buddies down.

Sometime later that day the doctor and a nurse came by, gave me a shot of something to deaden the pain and pulled out the piece of steel. It was about 3 inches long and just a sliver wide. He cleaned the wound and put two small stitches in to hold the entrance together. I did not keep the steel because he had thrown it out the door on a pile of similar items. But I did secure a couple of pieces of shrapnel that I was able to bring home with me. One of them is in the case with the medals.

The feet problem was another thing. The orderly turned out to be a guy from El Dorado. I did not know him, but it was like old home week as we found we had several mutual friends. He is the one that brought me the bad news. I will always remember the look on his face as he told me he had looked at the schedule and I was scheduled to have both my feet amputated the next morning. All I could think of was that I would be on crutches or in a wheel chair the rest of my life. I was in shock.

One of the other patients that had trench foot told me that his had started to peel between the good skin and the black gangrene. They had put off amputation until it was determined if the peeling would continue.

I took a look at my feet and there was a fairly definite line between the black and the white. I thought that if I could make it look like mine was peeling I could also get a postponement.

All night I tried to slide my fingernails under the black. I would run the fingernail along the black, use a Kleenex to wipe away the blood and pass the Kleenex down the row of bunks. The last man would put it in the trash close to the door. Gradually I began to see a little progress. By the time morning came I had made a nice neat little place that to me looked like the start of peeling. If only the doctor could be convinced.

The doctor came by and I showed him my handiwork. He had a funny look on his face, and I believe he knew what I had done. But, I also believe, he had so much to do that he decided to let the stateside doctors decide what to do. He put an evacuation order on my chart.

Later that morning a Major came by with a box full of Purple Heart medals and either put one on each pillow or pinned one to the gown. He said how proud the Army was of our participation in the war effort and that the award would be put in our files at a later date. (In my case, there was no entry in my file and all efforts to get it put in the file have been ignored).

I was taken back to Liege, Belgium and then by a four person ambulance through Aachen, Germany, Maastricht, Holland and into Amsterdam, Holland. From there we were flown on a C46 (military version of the DC3) to Glasgow, Scotland. There we were taken from the airfield to the harbor and put on board a converted luxury liner for transport to the States. This ship had been stripped of all its pretty goodies and fitted out with rows and rows of bunks. The most seriously wounded were put in the converted staterooms. The rest of us were put in the main cabin on the upper 2 or 3 levels. I was on the main deck at the rear (stern) of the ship. My bunk was very close to the big double doors that opened onto the open deck.

I had one more near miss.

I was on deck, standing by the railing off to the left, watching land disappear into the distance. We were well out of the harbor and under a full head of steam. Suddenly the alarm klaxon sounded and there was feverous activity. The loud speakers blared out the information that we were under sub attack and a missile had been fired. All hands at their stations. I went to the right side of the deck and there in the distance was the wake of a torpedo coming right for our ship. I thought "Will I make it this time?"

The ship was moving fast and the torpedo was coming straight for the ship. I thought to myself that there was a chance it would go behind us if we were moving fast enough. There was not time enough to find a place to hide, and I was not going to dig a foxhole through the deck. So I just stood there and watched it come. If it hit, the place of impact would be pretty close to directly under where I stood.

I held my breath.

It seemed like everything was moving in slow motion, but this torpedo did not outrun its target, nor did it score another in a long list of hits which the German subs had made.

There was barely twenty yards between the stern of the ship and the torpedo when it came even with us. It went hissing off into the distance to probably explode on a rock or piece of land somewhere in Northern Scotland.

In the meantime some American sub chaser aircraft were cruising around dropping some depth charges. We kept going and those of us who had witnessed this near miss could only speculate whether the sub lived to strike again.

We crossed the Atlantic in six days and landed in a safe harbor in Boston. It was Feb. 28th, 1945.

While I was being rushed to safety in the good ole USA, the 78th and my friends were moving down the Cologne plain towards the bridge at Remagen, where it crossed the Rhine River. They went on to cross the bridge just before and during its destruction by the fighter bombers of the German's. They continued on, taking and securing the Autobahn to open a path for the multitude of munitions and supplies needed to go on to finish the job. There were more battles, but it was just a matter of time.

In Berlin they were part of the occupation and were sent home in small groups, or sent of furloughs in Paris and London, or in a couple of cases, given a semester of study at Oxford. I wished I could have been with them.

Before we get too far away from the war zone, I must confess that I only told a small part of the experience. One that I would not care to repeat, but one that I would not take a million dollars for.

However, I would gladly do it all again if it would help maintain our precious freedoms. Until a person has seen the dark side of the human race in the form of the Hitler goals and what it would have been like under his yoke, that person can never realize what a priceless gift our forefathers in 1776 gave to all of us. It should, and must, be maintained at all costs—

Even with our lives.

A few of the things I left out and did not care to describe the details:

We were only a mile or so from the massacre of captured American troops at the hands of the Germans.

The smell of a belly wound.

The screams of a man trying to find his arm or leg that had been shot off.

The numbness of fingers that could not slide the frozen rifle bolt, the need to urinate on the breech so he could load more shells and go on fighting.

The horror of having to pull a dead body from a fox hole, because the ground was too frozen to dig your own foxhole.

The fear when the earth trembled and the air was filled with artillery and a hundred tanks are moving your way, bent of destruction.

The perverse joy you feel when you throw a grenade in a machine gun nest and the blast makes the nest go silent.

The utter exhaustion after an all day attack, moving inch by bloody inch, and the relief to dig a defense and to get a little sleep, no matter that there is about 2 inches of icy water and mud in the bottom.

The bliss of a clean dry pair of sox or long handled underwear.

I hope this can explain why I cannot understand a rational person that will not salute the flag, or stand at attention when one passes. It is at times like that when I wonder if it had all been worth it. Surely there is some little thought that if those funny old men had not done what they did when they were not yet 20, the world would not be the same. Most of us do not ask for thanks, only to respect and appreciate the life of freedom they have.

The funny thing, I was proud and pleased to be just a tiny part of this grand undertaking. Some day maybe your kids and grandkids will too.

There was much more, and I was only there for three months. Many were there for two or three years. They were the real heroes.

BACK IN THE GOOD OLE USA

So, here I am in Boston. It took most of a day to get us off the ship and to an Army hospital. I never did know the name of it. It was sort of an intermediate stop where we were examined by more doctors and then were to be sent to various hospitals where there was specific expertise in treating certain wounds and problems.

I was examined the next day and the doctors seemed to think that true enough, the feet seemed to be peeling and that we would have a little time to determine the next course of action. I was turned over to the USO and they told me that I could make some calls to my family and could make some local calls if there was anyone I would wish to contact.

Of course, I wanted to call my folks to tell them I had made it safely back to the USA. Also, I wanted to know how my brother Bill was coming along. Along with worrying about keeping my head down to avoid being shot at, the last letter from the folks I had received was a couple of days after Christmas telling me that Bill had a heart murmur and was going into the hospital. So, all that time, I did not know whether he was OK or not. They told me Bill was OK and they were glad that I was back away from the danger. I told them I would let them know how I fared with the feet, and would come home on furlough as soon as possible. I asked them to spread the word that I was basically OK.

The second call was local. Priscilla was the only one my age that had written with any regularity. She was now going to the "Garland School for Girls", a very exclusive finishing school for young ladies whose folks had the money to send them there. I do not believe they were too interested in filling their pretty heads with any heavy subjects. The girls were there primarily to further their education in how to conduct themselves in society, dress and groom themselves properly, and to learn tricks on how to catch a suitable husband. We had already determined that I was not suitable for a husband, but would do very well as a friend that had been in the War and was now a returned, wounded veteran. It had a certain ring to it I guess.

Anyhow, I called her and she rushed out to the hospital the next morning and spent the day with me. We caught up on all the news about her family (who I was fond of) and my experiences and her future plans. We ate in the cafeteria of the hospital since I could not move much except with crutches, and we sat in the day room and talked. She was attractive and I got ribbed a lot from everyone including the doctors and nurses. The USO group took our picture and we said goodbye. That was the last I saw of her.

It was a pleasant association and I learned a lot about how others outside Kansas and Missouri lived and thought. I learned even more about myself. The last two years had made me miss the upper teen experience. I had to grow up fast and hard. I passed go and went directly to adult.

Chapter 13

The Countdown to the Finale

But now we continue the saga.

The next day they shipped a group of us to a general hospital in Durham, North Carolina. I stayed there off and on assigned to the hospital for about 5 months.

My problem was my feet and legs. They immediately started the cure consisting of a penicillin shot every three hours and a cleaning of the feet and a layer of lanolin (grease derived from sheep wool). The penicillin was new then and they did not know how it would work long term. It must have done the job because I still have my feet. I do know that after about the first few days, the places they tried to give me the shot became very hard and it was difficult to get the needle inserted. They moved from place to place on my body trying to find a soft spot. The area was so hard that when they tried to insert the needle the needle would either break off or bend. After the three week schedule I was a mess, but still had my feet. That was the theme I told myself day after day—I still have my feet.

After the first six months I could get around pretty well and some of us took little jaunts into Durham to sight see. As time progressed, I could go further and further. I was always cautioned, however, that the feet and legs would never be the same again and that I would always have problems because the small blood veins were mostly destroyed by the gangrene.

At about the two month mark I was allowed to make the trip home. I could move around pretty well and could make the journey without too much trouble.

It was good to see the folks again and I stayed around the house for a few days just resting and visiting with neighbors. Then I started making a few calls to people I knew—mostly females since most of the men were still in the service or could not make it home. It was good duty being the only male (and a soldier) in the whole town of Eldorado. I made contact with several at the school house where my classmates were all enrolled in the Junior College there. We went to the lake and to the swimming pool and to the movies.

Too soon it was time to go back to Durham. I had made the trip in good shape and could relax and let the future take care of itself.

Those of us who were able to be up and about were issued passes so we could go to town almost every day. We toured Duke University and the countryside, which was a lot different than Kansas. We went to the local USO to the dances (which I could not participate it) and hung out listening to music and drinking cokes.

The feet were coming along so well that I was able to keep shoes and socks on most of the time. The toes were the last to heal and they kept me on hospital time longer than I thought was necessary.

Then, in about another month I was sent home on recuperative leave again. I really think they did not know what else to do with me. I was not going into combat again so would not be sent to the Pacific unless it was at a desk job.

This was when I met Dee (formerly) for the first time. She was a part of the group I had met and had hung out with on the first furlough. At that time she was going with Jim Carnes, a guy she had known for a long time and whose folks were friends of Dee's.

We went to the airport, which was so small that a small airplane took off once in a while. It was still wartime and gas was still in short supply. But we enjoyed this little diversion. We all went to the movies and did the usual things to do in a small town, which was not much.

The first time I really took an interest in Dee was when a group of us went to the Blue Moon Night Club in Wichita. I had a date with Jamie Mawson and Dee had a date with Jim Carnes. Several others were there also. We all danced with the each other—we were all just a bunch of good friends.

But something happened that changed my world. I was so taken with Dee that I had to take great pains to keep my interest from showing. After all, she had known J.C. for a long time and I was not going to interfere with that.

Then it was kicked up a notch when one by one the others all went off to College or back to the Service. We were the only two left.

Dee's Dad was the manager of the local Fox Theater and Dee was the cashier and helped him with the books. I would go to the theater just before the show was over and wait for her to close out the tickets and the books. I usually went in and watched the last of whatever was playing. I like to say that I have seen the last of more movies than most people have seen movies. Then we would go to Graves Drug Store on the next corner and have lemonade with plain water. Sorry, but we weren't heavy drinkers.

Then on June 7, 1945 Dee kissed me and said "Happy Birthday Honey". And that was all it took. I had tried not to come between her and whoever she may have been serious about. We had not even kissed goodnight up to that point. But, from there on it was just a matter of time. What we did not know at the time was that we would have a 46 month engagement. The problem was that there were several things that had to be done first.

I had to finish up my commitment to the Army. VE day had come and gone, but there was still Japan to take care of. It had not been decided yet whether I would be discharged or kept on until the bitter end. After that I would have a College Degree to get. So, while we were not content to let things stand, we accepted it.

Dee still had some schooling to take care of also, and up to that point she had never really thought seriously about marriage to anyone. She had to think about it a bit, and I had to go have that interview with her Dad. We explained to her folks that we cared about each other and eventually wanted to get married, but were putting it off until all matters were either settled or planned for. They gave us their blessing.

As soon as I returned to Durham, they packed me up and sent me to a redistribution center in Hot Springs, Arkansas. This was where they sent those who had been in hospitals to be re-evaluated and the determination was made as to what they would do with us.

Hot Springs was, and is, a resort town. It is full of spas made possible by the natural hot springs in the area. We stayed in the very best hotels, although they had been altered from very deluxe to 2 to 4 bunks per room. They were still a lot better than we had been used to for the past 2 years. We basically had the freedom to roam wherever we wanted and to take advantage of the hot baths and massages—which we did daily. The only thing we had to do was appear for roll call each morning and watch the bulletin boards and listen to the special announcements for other formations, activities, interviews, etc. On one of those formations we all received the Combat Infantry Badge.

We could take busses to various scenic spots and to nearby lakes for boating, etc. We spent about 3 weeks there before going to our next post.

First though, we had another short furlough. Since it is not too far from Hot Springs to Eldorado, I took advantage of seeing everyone again.

Then, another bus to Tyler, Texas and Camp Fannin, where I was assigned duty in the department that took care of all the service records of those stationed at Camp Fannin. It was a cushy job.

My job was supervision over the files from A to M. We had regular hours, did not have to do any training, did not have to stand formations or guard duty, and did not have to eat in the regular mess hall. There was a special one for the non-coms (that's from Corporal to First Sergeant).

While there, we had special permanent passes that allowed us off base after 5 pm and all day Saturday and Sunday. This was different than we were used to which was standing in line for a single pass every single time we wanted to leave the base.

I became acquainted with Vic Krentz and his wife Mary Lou. I spent a lot of time with them. They lived off the base in an apartment. Another one of the men in my barracks was a sports nut and owned a motorcycle. I had sworn never to ride one, but he convinced me that he would be very safe because he used it only for transportation and not wild rides. His bike was basically a two seater. There was a second saddle with a bar to hang onto. We cruised over a good portion of Northern Texas. One of the things we did was go to a football game in Tyler. We learned that the Texans were fanatic about their football—especially in Tyler where they had almost always had a team in the top ten in the Nation, even in War time. They were equally as gung-ho about their Cheerleaders. They went to all the contests and were also rated near the top. It was pretty obvious that they were picked for their beauty. There were probably 50 girls either leading the cheers, or in groups doing stunts and working their way up to cheerleader.

This one game was attended by a contingent from Camp Fannin. There must have been at least a hundred of us. We were seated on the 50 yard line but near the top of the bleachers. It was a beautiful day and we were all eager for the day's activities. But the activities were not what we bargained for.

The marching band made a complicated formation and came to a halt in front of the bleachers and played the Star Spangled Banner. Probably 25% of the people in the bleachers stood at attention took their hats off and placed their hand over their heart. The rest of them talked and yelled greetings to others, kept their hats on and were not at all interested. And this was still during the war. We were seething. But it was nothing compared to the next thing the band did—they played "The Eyes of Texas Are Upon You". Off came the hats, everyone stood at attention and everyone sang along with the music. That was more than we could stand. They knew we were there and were deliberately being obnoxious. One of the soldiers shouted to us to sing our version of the song. So with the band playing and the Texan's sing their song, we sang along with the version that we had used many times in our marching. I will not repeat the words since a lot of them were profane, but it did cause some excitement. Fist fights broke out and then there was a free for all. Most of the students were the younger guys that were not old enough for the service, and the usual smattering of 4F's.

We were giving a pretty good account of ourselves and thoroughly disrupted their little Texan party. The band scattered and a lot of those who had dished the Flag and National Anthem had bloody noses, or worse.

Some MP's were there and did not make too much of an effort to stop it. All of the soldiers then left the field together and went back to the camp. One of the guys who worked on the camp newspaper wrote up the incident and suggested that the military should boycott all games. To his credit, the Lt. General in charge of the base made a formal protest to Tyler High School and told the authorities there that the Tyler campus was now off limits. That put a real roadblock in front of a lot of the younger soldiers who had struck up friendships with the girls in the school. There was a lot of grumbling.

Another sporting event we went to was entirely different. The PGA was having a tournament in the Dallas area. I was not into golf so do not recall the course or who was playing. I do remember the fantastic reception we received as we came up to the clubhouse. There were passes to all of the sponsor tents; we could eat (free) in the dining room and at any of the refreshment tents. Again, there must have been a hundred of us and they broke us into groups of 10 and each group was guided by a volunteer who stayed with us the whole time so we would not miss any goodies. They also saw to it that we met the golfers, and we had a front row around the greens. There were a group of musicians at one of the tents playing basically Dixieland music. After we arrived, they played a lot of military music. The truth of the matter, which we did not relate to them, was we had heard a lot of military music recently and appreciated the Dixieland and the popular swing music.

Back at Camp Fannin, our futures were being determined. It had been established that 84 points were needed to be honorably discharged from military duty. I had about 80 at that time. Some of the older guys were going home. There was one farewell after another. Some of them elected to stay in and make the military a career. At one time I thought that I would go that way. But I had now met Dee and knowing how the military works, I did not think that we would be happy that way.

Several interesting things happened. The war was still being fought in the Pacific. We had been victorious in a couple of big battles and had decimated the Japanese fleet. But they still held a big chunk of the Far East and the people they had captured, both civilian and military, were being treated badly. POW's were routinely beaten and starved. It was being discovered that there were medical factories where prisoners were used as test subjects for different diseases, mostly without benefit of anything to take away the pain. We were all happy when Aug. 6th, 1945 we dropped the atomic bomb on Hiroshima. Then on Aug. 9th, we dropped another one on Nagasaki. They really should have dropped one on Tokyo and Yokohama. Anyway, on September 2, 1945 the Japs surrendered to McArthur on the US Battleship Missouri in Tokyo Bay. VJ was here and the fighting ended. After 2,194 days of war, we were at peace.

Now it was certain that I would be going home before very long. So the evaluations picked up. Our section was busy updating and closing out the files. And most important of all, the points to get out had been dropped from 84 to 80. I now qualified, but I would not happen immediately because of the tremendous amount of people that had to be processed. The ones that had been in the most recent battles and the wounded were to go home first. Those of us who had fought overseas were next, and those who had been on the US mainland the whole time came last.

I had one more trip to make—make that two more. The first one was to Ft. MacArthur in southern California for discharge. I was moved there on Oct. 26.

While waiting for my number to be called, I worked in the Base Commander's office. My job was another easy one. I was in charge of the Officer's activities and checked them in and out of the Base, kept the roster by rank, made up their passes, made sure the cook in the Officer's mess hall (excuse me, their dining room) was kept advised of the numbers for each meal, etc. etc.

I was issued my own jeep so I could run errands for the Commander and anything else that needed done. Such as getting a supply of booze when there was a party at the BOQ (Bachelor Officer Quarters). The supply place for this was in San Louis Obispo.

I ate in the officer's dining room, but was not invited to the parties. I could sleep in while the ones in training would have to get up at dawn for the day's activities. I started the day with steak for breakfast.

I was still waiting for my time, at Christmas time. Since there was not that much use for my scintillating presence, they sent me home on another leave.

Dee and I were able to make some more plans. I had to start school and she had to continue her last two years, we talked it over and over. I had decided that I would like to work in radio. The two best schools in the country at that time for radio (and the just being developed TV) were Cornell and University of Denver.

It was interesting that DU also was a very prominent school for Art. Since Dee had been doing art all her life and wanted a degree in Fine Arts we made a tentative agreement to go to DU.

The GI bill had been established and I knew that it would pay for my way, but Dee's situation was different. Money would be a problem, but we thought that after the first semester she could probably get a scholarship to continue.

With that more or less decided I went back to Ft. MacArthur and stayed until Feb. 12, 1946, where I received my Honorable Discharge from the U.S. Army.

Another ex-soldier and I took a bus and went towards Kansas via Denver, where I stopped by to visit Aunt Pruda and Uncle Russell. Then on to Eldorado.

So, 976 days of my life came to an end. I have tried to share some of my thoughts and experiences with you. It reminds me of a funny paper strip. In it, the family takes out their secret weapon to put their kids to sleep. It was a telephone call to dear old dad who recounted some of his war exploits and the kids fell asleep right away.

SLEEP TIGHT

The following was written by George Mitchell; George was one of the 12 men that more or less were together throughout their Military careers. The story of these men was written by John McGugan and edited, proof read, and co-written by Jim Leek.

CITIZEN SOLDIERS
BELGIUM-GERMANY
1944 & 1945

FANFARE FOR THE COMMON MAN
DEDICATED TO MY COMRADES, COMBAT
INFANTRYMEN, IN THE 78TH LIGHTNING
DIVISION, ALL HEROES IN THEIR OWN RIGHT.

SOLDIER IN THE RAIN
YOUNG LONESOME SOLDIER—SLEEPING IN THE RAIN
FAR FROM HOME-HALF A CHILD AND HALF A HERO
TOSSED BY THE TIMES—CAUGHT IN THE WINDS.

DREAM LONESOME SOLDIER-WEARY OF THE RAIN
DREAM OF HOME—SOMEONE'S SON, SOMEONE'S LOVER.
DREAM THAT YOUR SOMEDAY CHILD
NEVER KNOWS THE RAIN.

WE FOUGHT IN THE ARDENNES—THE BATTLE
OF THE BULGE—THE RHINELAND—THE REMAGEN
BRIDGEHEAD—CENTRAL EUROPE—AND ONTO
VICTORY AND ATONEMENT.

EACH AND EVERY ONE OF US A CHILD
OF DEMOCRACY